THE ENEMY WITHIN

The Enemy Within.

by

Oluwakemi Ola-Ojo © 2012

THE ENEMY WITHIN

1st Printing 2012
THE ENEMY WITHIN
ISBN: 978-1-908-015-11-2
© 2012 by Oluwakemi O. Ola-Ojo
All publishing rights belong exclusively to Protokos Publishers.

Published by,
Protokos Publishers
London
United Kingdom

Protokos Publishers -'Impacting our community through sharing'

Website: www.protokospublishers.co.uk
E-Mail: admin@protokospublishers.co.uk

Cover design:
'Guard your heart above all else, for it determines the course of your life.'
Proverbs 4:23 NLV ©2007

Printed in the United Kingdom. All rights reserved under International Copyright Law. Contents and/or cover may not be reproduced in whole or in part in any form without the express written consent of the Publisher.

ACKNOWLEDGEMENT

*I am most grateful to God, who through
The blessed Holy Spirit
Has been my teacher, friend and mentor.*

*I am grateful to God for my family, friends and,
The various Ministers who have been a blessing and
encouragement to me over the years*

*Thanks to my Editor, Mrs. `Sumbo Oladipo,
for editing this book.*

*Thanks to all who found time to read and
comment on this book,
For their invaluable comments and encouragements.*

*Finally but not in the least,
To the wonderful team at Protokos Publishers
For working round the clock to get this book published
and market my books.*

THE ENEMY WITHIN

CONTENTS

Acknowledgement		v
Introduction		viii
Chapter 1	Parent/Child	11
Chapter 2	Siblings	19
Chapter 3	Spouses	28
Chapter 4	In-laws	35
Chapter 5	Colleagues	39
Chapter 6	Bosses, Managers or Employers	45
Chapter 7	Neighbours	50
Chapter 8	Wicked Leaders	54
Chapter 9	Sickness and Poverty	59
Chapter 10	Self	69
Chapter 11	Selected Poems	85
Other books by the Author		111
Useful Addresses		130

THE ENEMY WITHIN

INTRODUCTION

An enemy as described by the 'Encarta Dictionary: English UK', is an unfriendly opponent who hates or seeks to harm somebody or something. It can also be a person or group especially military force that fights against another in combat or battle or a hostile nation or power. It can also be something that harms or opposes something else. It is an adversary or foe or rival.

The word 'Within' refers to something or someone in close proximity to another. It can also be described as being inside something or someone or for something or someone to be surrounded by another.

Simply put this book seeks to identify some unsuspected or confirmed enemies of the child of God, their roles or patterns of manifestation and the remedies available to a child of God in putting such enemies at bay so that they do not continue to pose a threat to them .

A popular African adage says, *'Ti iku ile koba pani to de kole pani.'*, By interpretation, this means that it is impossible for you to fall prey to external danger if you have not first been a victim of internal betrayal.

When the Holy Spirit gave me the title and the idea of this book, I could neither imagine nor think about the evils an enemy could do to an uninformed person, especially an unsuspecting child of God but one by one, the Holy Spirit began to teach and remind me of such instances in the Bible. According to Hosea 4:6, God's people are destroyed for lack of knowledge. .

Equally many people are ignorant of the world in which we live in – a world full of physical and spiritual battles. Unfortunately, ignorance is not an excuse in any court of law. All ignorance gets paid for one way or the other!

The aim of this book is not to bring fear to you or to make you suspicious of anyone but to enlighten, educate and empower you to be conscious of some of the various types of enemies that loiter within and around us, how they present themselves and how to equip yourself so that you do not become a victim through ignorance or carelessness.

The Bible in 1 Peter 5:8 admonishes the Christian to 'Be sober, be vigilant; because your adversary the devil, as a roaring lion, walks about, seeking whom he may devour' [American KJV]. In like manner, the book of Job tells us that Satan parades the world 24/7 going to and fro *[Job 1: 6-7]*.

THE ENEMY WITHIN

Although Satan is finite and can only be at one location at a time, he uses as many of his followers i.e. those who yield themselves to him to perform havoc simultaneously worldwide. But thanks to God, we have a remedy for him for 'When the enemy shall come in like a flood, the Spirit of the Lord shall lift up a standard against him' *[Isaiah 59:19].*

The subject of this book is restricted to the enemies identified in the Bible and they have been discussed in no particular order. However, it is necessary for us to recognize that our list is just to serve as a template for identifying enemies within and is therefore not exhaustive as there could be and possibly there are more enemies than those identified listed in this book.

It is my prayer that you would be blessed as you read.

CHAPTER 1

PARENT/CHILD

For the son dishonoureth the father, the daughter riseth up against her mother, the daughter in law against her mother in law; a man's enemies are the men of his own house. [Micah 7:6 (KJV)].

It is an aberration for a parent to kill their child and vice versa. Under normal circumstances, there should be an automatic parental care and love flowing from a parent to a child while a child should naturally love and respect the parent. However, it is not uncommon to find an unending row and enmity building up between a parent and the child.

And there are instances where the Bible does not identify a row or enmity between parent and child, yet the act of the parent to the child is just like that of the enemy. Let us examine one of such parents.

Athaliah

[2 Kings 8: 26, 11:1-23, 2; Chronicles 22 & 23 and 24:7]. According to the accounts given in the texts above,

PARENT/CHILD

Queen Athaliah was the daughter of King Ahab and Queen Jezebel. Her father, Ahab, was adjudged to have been the most wicked king in Israel while Jezebel her mother was evil personified. Both parents were known for their wickedness and were eventually destroyed by God for plotting the death of Naboth and unlawfully taking possession of his vineyard. Athaliah was married to a king and so became a queen. She was the mother of Ahaziah, king of Judah. Unfortunately, King Ahaziah died before his mother in a battle against King Jehu. In an unprecedented act of treason from mother to son, Athaliah embarked on a killing spree, killing all her grandsons (except one that was hidden), amongst whom was the rightful heir to the throne. Thereafter, Athaliah enthroned herself as Queen and as shocking as it may seem, she ruled Judah for six full years! That is, until she was killed and dethroned in the seventh year of her reign.

The untimely death of any parent or benefactor can expose a child to lack of care from jealous or wicked relatives. No one knows when, where and how they will die. Therefore as parents, it is necessary for us to put a comprehensive plan in place to take care of our children in case of any unforeseen circumstance including death. Such plans could include different forms of insurance, bank deposits, adequate will, determining the transfer of our properties to our children as well as good trusteeship.

The account of Athaliah teaches us that the fact that someone is your parent or grandparent does not mean they may not harbour evil against you or even attempt to take your life. Many parents and grandparents have sacrificed their offspring to the devil in search of power, money and position in the occult world. They care less so long as they get their desired position, power or money. Many parents and grandparents have killed the star, talent in their child or grandchild whilst some other wicked ones have rendered their child or grandchild impotent or regressive academically, career wise, in their marriage or physically so they can have that child or grand child to themselves alone. They put their selfish need above the child or grandchild's legitimate rights and needs.

May the Lord deliver you and I from such demon possessed parent or grandparent in Jesus' name. You may wish to say this prayer for yourself:

Prayer points:

- ❖ Oh Lord, please protect my parents and all the destiny helpers assigned to help me from any untimely death. I refuse to see evil in Jesus' name.
- ❖ Lord, please deliver me from all untimely death instigated by my parents or grandparents. Father, please help me not to be a casualty of any war in Jesus' name.
- ❖ Lord, assign Your angels to protect me day and night from every trap of my enemies. Lord I refuse to die before my time in Jesus' name.
- ❖ Lord, please deliver me from any wicked

grandparents or parents.

❖ Lord, please permanently silent every evil power or force whose existence is a real threat to my living and achieving Your divine purpose for my life.

❖ Lord, in Your majesty, please dethrone every person or power occupying my rightful position. Lord in Your name I reclaim every lost throne and glory in Jesus' name.

❖ Oh Lord, empower me with the wisdom, protection and provision needed for my God assigned duties in Jesus' name I pray with thanksgiving.

CHILD TO PARENT

In an ideal world, the child ought to love, respect and honour the parents enough to protect them especially in their old age or when the parents now become vulnerable. Unfortunately some parents for whatever reasons get physically killed by their children – the very ones they birthed, washed, fed, trained and loved. Other parents may not be physically killed by their children but emotionally, psychologically, mentally or financially killed or destroyed. A child that sets himself or herself to commit horrible atrocities or be involved in unspeakable crimes may be leading the parents to all manners of diseases including high blood pressure or sending them to an early grave. Here are some examples of such children:

King Sennacherib of Assyria

In 2 Kings 18:13-19:34, King Sennacherib laid a siege against King Hezekiah of Judah. In his military campaign against King Hezekiah, King Sennacherib disrespected the King of kings and the Lord of lords by his words and threats to King Hezekiah and the people of Judah. All attempts to settle with King Sennacherib failed as he refused to accept all that was offered to him.

Then King Hezekiah and the people sought the face of the Lord and God sent them word through Isaiah the prophet who assured King Hezekiah of God's promise to step into the battle and to deal with King Sennacherib. In the night the angel of the Lord went into King Sennacherib's camp and killed 185,000 members of his army. The following day, King Sennacherib had news of an army invading his own city so he returned home to his capital of Nineveh and stayed there. God defended and protected Judah as He (the Lord) had spoken through Prophet Isaiah. But one day while King Sennacherib was worshiping in the temple of his god Nisroch, his sons Adrammelech and Sharezer killed him with their swords. They then escaped to the land of Ararat, and another son, Esarhaddon, became the next king of Assyria. For King Sennacherib, his death was as spoken by God through His prophet. His sons had access to him and they knew where to find him at the temple of his god.

PARENT/CHILD

King David and his sons

When King David murdered Uriah and took Bathsheba his wife, he opened himself and his family to wars within his household [2 Samuel 11- 12:10]. How many parents have exposed their families and children, some to generations yet unborn as a consequence of curses or imposed yokes and burden.

King David had many sons among whom were Absalom and Adonijah. Absalom was King David's third son and Adonijah was his fourth son. Each had at various times raised their armies to dethrone King David. Absalom drove King David out of Jerusalem and fought his father but God defended King David against his sons and they each died. What kept King David alive from being killed by his sons was God's covenant with him of protection and defence.

What sinful door have you opened into your family - that of lies, wickedness, uncaring attitude, selfishness, greed, unlawfulness, disloyalty, enmity to God and man. We have to be careful as parents regarding the way we live our lives, for every act, thought and deed of ours is a seed and we will surely reap what we sow, here on earth if the Lord tarries and in eternity when we have ended our sojourn on planet earth. 'Be not deceived; God is not mocked: for whatever a man sows, that shall he also reap [Galatians 6:7. American KJV].

How have you raised your children? – To love God and other people? To save lives or to destroy others? What examples have you passed on to your children? What is your relationship with God? Can God go all the way to fight your battle against your children should they attempt to do the same thing like Absalom? [2 Samuel 22].

There is no perfect parent. It is not uncommon for us to offend the spirit of our children, wounding them beyond our imaginations. We need to be humble enough to seek for forgiveness and reconciliation. With such child or grandchild, open communication permits progress. We need to stop sweeping things and issues under the carpet. As we prayerfully talk about such issues with them, we create an atmosphere of understanding, forgiveness and togetherness. For parents who feel vulnerable and are afraid of being killed by their children, please pray, using these prayer points if you do not already have yours. Equally seek for professional help without any further delay. from E.g. the police, a Christian counsellor or pastor.

Prayer points:
- ❖ Oh Lord, please forgive me of any wrong doing as a parent that might cause my children's anger towards me.
- ❖ Lord, for any act of bad, wrong or wicked parenting, do kindly forgive me.

PARENT/CHILD

- ❖ Lord, please grant me Your forgiveness and that of my children.
- ❖ Father, please grant me favour in the sight of my children.
- ❖ In my vulnerable status, please help that my children, close associates and those I have been a blessing to in times past be not the one that will kill me in Jesus name.
- ❖ Lord, in Your mercy, please grant that my children show me kindness and mercy.
- ❖ Father, I refuse any untimely death through our children in Jesus' name have I prayed and with thanksgiving (Amen)

CHAPTER 2

SIBLINGS

And a man's foes shall be they of his own household.
[Matthew 10:36-37 (KJV)]

Sibling rivalry is something that is common in a lot of families and more often than not, it is taken for granted. Although healthy rivalry amongst siblings sometimes has positive effects and in some cases serves as impetus and motivation for children to excel in their studies for example, the truth is, such rivalry could become unhealthy and get out of hands, leading to grave consequences if not checked and nipped in the bud. Unhealthy rivalry amongst siblings sometimes gets so bad and has been known to result in one sibling killing another. When sibling rivalry gets to this level, it can only be prayerfully dealt with.

Cain and Abel
[Genesis 4:1-10]
Cain and Abel were brothers born of the same parents – Adam and Eve. As a matter of fact, some Bible theologians have proferred that they were twins, because it was not recorded that Adam knew his wife a second time when the birth of Abel was mentioned. In the course of their adult life each of them chose his career and brought a sacrifice to God from his proceeds. While Abel's sacrifice

of the firstlings of his flock to God was accepted, Cain's hamper of fruits was rejected by God. Cain became angry, God warned him against his wrong attitude and gave him another chance to correct his sacrifice but Cain did not take this offer. Instead he lured unsuspecting Abel into the field and murdered him [Genesis 4:8].

If in your family you are the only one that is doing very well and your siblings are not, despite them having the same upbringing and opportunity like you, be wise, for you may have become the envy of the family including your siblings. Make God your Father and protector and apply godly discernment to know how to walk in and out amongst them. And when it is imperative for you to move with them, then it is advisable that others know of your whereabouts.

Stories abound of people have been ruined or made bankrupt by the mismanagement of their business ventures that they have assigned to family members or associates who really did not have their interest at heart. Anything or anyone that takes away another person's means of livelihood is an enemy. We ought to be careful who we entrust with our lives, properties and business ventures.

Joseph and his older half brothers
Joseph was the son of Jacob through Rachael, his preferred wife. He was born to Jacob in his old age and after many years of Rachael's barrenness. Rachael

eventually died prematurely while giving birth to Benjamin, Joseph's younger brother. It is therefore understandable that Jacob had a soft spot for Joseph and preferred him above his ten older half-brothers. Jacob also made Joseph a coat of many colours signifying his being chosen and favoured above the first ten sons! He was like their father's life line!

Joseph being a child was unable to interpret the consequences of his father's preference for him, a situation he worsened by being cocky and showy in his early years. Coupled with this, Joseph was gifted in dreams; a gift he also handled immaturely. Every time he had a dream he was quick to share it with his siblings and parents. These dreams made him even more unpopular in his household.

There is a lesson to be learnt here. There is need to tread carefully when sharing our dreams and visions because it is not everybody that wishes us well and is interested in seeing our dreams come true. On the contrary, many would rather we perish with our dreams unfulfilled! There is therefore need to ask God to grant you an excellent spiritual antenna that will help you feel the spiritual atmosphere of the places where you operate. Whether you believe it or not, there are many dream killers out there and in our midst.

So it was on a certain day, Jacob sent Joseph to visit his ten older brothers in the field to check their welfare and

SIBLINGS

bring back word to him. Joseph travelled many days to get to his brothers' settlement. On getting there, he discovered they had moved to another place – Dothan and, off he went again in search of them *[Genesis 37:12-17].*

Seeing Joseph afar off, his brothers said 'here comes the dreamer, let us kill him and see what will become of his dreams'. They hated him and could not withstand his dreams. They desperately wanted to kill him for his dreams and in the hope that they might be able to tamper with his future and terminate his destiny because they could not imagine him ruling over them. They neither appreciated his efforts of travelling so far, the stress involved nor the potential dangers he had faced to bring them word from their father; they ignored the message and did not fear the one who sent the message. They disrespected Rachael's memory and did not love Joseph or show him mercy. Not once did they think of giving him a second chance. No, they did not consider his youth (Joseph at this time was just a teenager, history records that he was 17). They detested his very existence and place in the family. At their best they dumped him in an empty well and sat down to a good meal, making merry whilst he cried all night in the dry and dark well. They cared less if he was bitten by scorpions, snakes or any poisonous insect, they neither offered him food, nor warmth nor water, but rather, took his robe of identity, protection and comfort. In the morning, naked and without food or water, they sold him into slavery to their cousins for twenty pieces of silver! *[Genesis 37: 18-28].*

Are you planning to kill or sell anyone into the slavery of life or expose them to the wolves of the world, the occult inclusive? Or have you been sold into slavery for sex or forced labour by your siblings? Or have you been physically, emotionally or spiritually attacked by your siblings or their agent?

To any wicked sibling, it is never too late to retrace your steps and release that brother or sister because while you may be able to fight a God-given dream, you will never win or prosper in your evil doing. Now, today and right now is the chance for you to confess your wickedness and make your ways right with God and your siblings. Today as you hear God's voice do not harden your heart. God knows it all and sees it all and you cannot hide from Him *[Hebrews 3:7, 15, 4:7b].*

If on the other hand you are like Joseph may I suggest that you amend your ways with God and hold on steadfastly to God your Maker, the One who does not and cannot lie, the One who knows the end before the beginning, the One who is able to deliver you from all the evil around, the One whose plans for your life cannot be aborted or destroyed, the One who is able to make any and every situation including yours work for your good for as long as you love Him and are called according to His purpose, the One who will not grant the request of the enemy over your life, the One who gave you the dream and wrote the script of your life. If God be for you no one dead or alive, single or multiple can successfully be against you. Hang in there with God and He will make sure that your enemy's counsel or enterprise against you will not prosper in Jesus' Name *[Romans 8:31]*.

Jehoram and his brothers
Jehoram succeeded his father Jehoshaphat as the king of Judah after his death. Jehoshaphat before he died gave great gifts of silver, gold, precious things and fenced cities in Judah to his sons – Azariah, Jehiel, Zechariah, Azariah, Michael and Shephaiah. Jehoshaphat however gave the Kingdom of Judah to Jehoram his first son. In the wickedness of Jehoram's heart he killed all his brothers once he became the king after the home call of Jehoshaphat *[2 Chronicles 21:1-6]*.

Jehoram for whatever reasons killed his innocent brothers who were not mentioned in the Bible as being a threat to him whatsoever. Perhaps so that he could feel more secured on the throne without any of his brothers who could challenge him later on in his reign. Killing to secure your throne or position is evil and wicked.

Absalom and Amnon
Parents who miss or refuse to discipline their children when they have done wrong things against God or humanity leave such children to receive 'jungle justice' from those whom they have offended. As parents we must not be afraid to seek the face of the Lord, ask for

THE ENEMY WITHIN

godly counsel and tackle our children's misbehaviour head-on. Failure to do so means we do not love our children and we do not obey God's instructions in *Proverbs 29:15, 3:11-12* and the scripture that says that the Lord disciplines everyone He loves *[Hebrews 12:6]*. When we are afraid of our children we are setting them up for a destructive future and expecting sorrow when 'jungle justice' is applied.

Amnon was the eldest son of King David, born in Hebron. His mother was Ahinoam the Jezreelitess *(II Samuel 3:2)*. Lusting after his half-sister Tamar, who was very beautiful, he lured her to his quarters by feigning illness and requesting her to prepare his food; he then raped her and cast her out *(II Samuel 13:1-14)*. When King David heard of this he was very angry but did not punish or discipline Amnon. However, Tamar's brother Absalom, enraged by Amnon's treatment of his sister, swore to avenge her *(II Samuel 13:15-22)*. Two years later Absalom invited Amnon and all the other royal princes to a sheep shearing celebration at his estate at Baal Hazor. When Amnon's heart was merry with wine Absalom ordered his men to kill him *(II Samuel 13:23-33)* and he then fled to Talmai, the son of the king of Geshur *(II Samuel 13:34-38)*.

If as a parent, you are blessed with more than a child, may I suggest that you spend quality time praying against sibling rivalry? Address and rebuke any wayward child's behavior. We must train and teach our children in every aspect of life using our past mistakes where applicable. Our children when properly taught and instructed should not repeat our mistakes. Avoid showing favouritism, however little or insignificant you consider it to be. Avoid setting the children up one against the other – in other words do not play 'divide and rule.'

And if you are experiencing challenging sibling rivalry or jealousy, may I ask you to say this prayer:

Prayer points:
- ❖ Oh Lord, please forgive me all my sins, words and actions that might make my other siblings jealous of me.
- ❖ Lord, please help me to have the right attitude to my other siblings. As a star in my family, may my family never have to mourn over me. Lord I will not die before my time in Jesus' name [2 Samuel 1:21].
- ❖ Father, in Your mercy I pray against every form of negative sibling rivalry in Jesus' name.
- ❖ Father, please protect me from every sibling rivalry and jealousy in Jesus' name.
- ❖ Lord, please expose every evil/wicked plan that any of my siblings or family might be setting up for me.
- ❖ Lord, irrespective of my sibling's attitude towards me, may all Your promises for my life materialize in Jesus' name even in their presence.

❖ Father, in your mercy, help me to show an unconditional love to my siblings in Jesus' name have I prayed and with thanksgiving [Amen].

Seek the face of God asking for mercy and wisdom. Seek for godly counselling.

CHAPTER 3
SPOUSES

"So went Satan forth from the presence of the LORD, and smote Job with sore boils from the sole of his foot unto his crown. And he took him a potsherd to scrape himself withal; and he sat down among the ashes. Then said his wife unto him, Dost thou still retain thine integrity? Curse God, and die."
[Job 2:7-9 (KJV)]

"But there was none like unto Ahab, which did sell himself to work wickedness in the sight of the LORD, whom Jezebel his wife stirred up."
[1 Kings 21:25-26 (KJV)]

"Now the name of the man was Nabal; and the name of his wife Abigail: and she was a woman of good understanding, and of a beautiful countenance: but the man was churlish and evil in his doings; and he was of the house of Caleb."
[1 Samuel 25:3-4 (KJV)]

Husband
Ideally people marry the love of their lives. Part of the vow in any culture is for the couple to protect each other till death separates them. Unfortunately there are instances when the husband lets down the wife or vice

versa. Let's examine two of such:

A Levite in *Judges 19:1-29* was faced with some homosexuals who wanted to sleep with his host and himself. This Levite gave his wife to these whores to sleep with her all night. By the time these wicked men had abused this innocent woman, she died outside the door of where her husband was with her hands on the threshold. This Levite could have taken counsel from his servant earlier on where to spend the night but he didn't, ignoring a valuable counsel. This Levite willingly gave his wife to heartless, godless and fearless men to 'do to her what seemeth good unto them' whilst his own life was spared *[Judges 19:24]*.

Any man who knowingly exposes his wife or children or anyone in his care to become prostitutes or turns them over to any godless person or persons to do to them what seems good unto such heartless men is an enemy of that woman or child.

How many have used their wives or children or parents to make money or donated them to the occult to be physically, verbally, emotionally or spiritually abused? How many have turned their innocent daughter, niece, younger cousin, sibling or maid into their sleeping partner forgetting that God sees it and knows about their evil acts and intents. These heartless people have no thought about the effects and consequences of their abuse on the lives of those they abuse

THE ENEMY WITHIN

To any evil perpetrator may I remind you of the words of a song that says:

> *You cannot hide it from God*
> *You may cover your sins*
> *So that no one may know*
> *But you cannot hide from God.*

How many women and perhaps men, die unnecessarily daily trying to stay married in an abusive relationship? It is not worth it my sister, it is not worth it my brother. Seek for help and you do not have to lose your life in any relationship either. Don't stay in that abusive relationship, daily making excuses for your molesting spouse. The fact that you married a wrong person should not be seen as more than making a costly mistake based perhaps on a wrong judgment or expectation. Don't become someone's slave, punch bag or door mat when you can return to your family who will love you unconditionally and to God – your Creator who will make a way of escape for you *[Judges 19:1-2]*. What is your worth to your husband? Is he to you like Jesus Christ is to the Church who protects and love his church like his bride?

Turning your spouse into a prostitute or drug addict is a sure way to kill them. Your wife is a weaker vessel that needs to be appreciated, treasured and properly looked after, not otherwise. Brother, what is the worth of your wife to you? Do you unconditionally love her and help her or are you making her to pay for the sins of your ex-girlfriends or partners or mother or sister? Are you your wife's enemy or friend, lover, protector and provider?

Wife
Ideally a wife is created to be a help meet not a rival or destiny competitor or anointing destroyer *[Genesis 2:18-20]*. Whilst some men are made in marriage, some others are destroyed by their wrong choices and the manifestation of such women later in the relationship. Prayerfully carrying one's immediate family along when making this choice especially in a family that has the love and interest of the man at heart can be very helpful. A wife/woman that is so superficial, wealth conscious, speaks to and is very friendly with one's enemies may be on a mission to kill the man or other members of his family. There is a wise saying that a friend to an enemy is an enemy.

Our God's assigned purpose, assignment and destiny can be enhanced or otherwise by whom we are married to. Samson's taste for the strange women invariably led to his untimely death. His parents warned him but he brushed their warnings aside and disregarded their godly counsel *[Judges 14:1-3, 15-17, 16:14-16]*. The warning signs were written all over from the very beginning of the relationship but he did not take them serious enough to pull out or back off from a disastrous relationship with the strange woman – Delilah.

THE ENEMY WITHIN

Strong and anointed as he was, he allowed his sexual gratification, 'few minutes' pleasure to put him into permanent darkness, pain, bondage and ridicule. He lost his vision, mission and anointing and died childless. How many have disregarded the counsel of God and perhaps their family and gone ahead into relationships that invariably led them to a 'dead end' of hurts, heart aches, lack of fulfilment, disappointments, untold failures and all manner of abuse and some unfortunately, death.

As we have men who abuse their wives so we have men who are abused physically, mentally, emotionally, financially by their wives. Be wary of any woman however beautiful or 'satisfying' she is who seeks to find out your strength in order to use it against you. Any woman or person who seeks to indulge you more in your weakness or disrespect or discourage your strength or anointing is an enemy with whom you should have no business.

Anything or anyone that threatens your life or existence is an enemy for which you need godly counsel, prayers and action. Many men out of shame have stayed with abusive partners and some of them have been killed by such partners. If this sounds like you, please do all that you can and that is possible now and walk out of that relationship alive because shame has no gender. Do not listen to satanic lies or be fooled by the crocodile tears or 'the sweet talk' of your spouse.

SPOUSES

How many have claimed that they will be able to change their spouse after the marriage? Brother with your eyes wide open physically and spiritually sound, seek the face of the Lord, seek His voice and commandments. Remember you will have to live with your choice and its consequences. Does she unconditionally accept you and in love obey you or does she make you pay for the sins of her ex-boyfriends or ex-partners?

If you have married the wrong spouse or your spouse's attitude has now turned into something negative then you may wish to pray along these lines:

Prayer Points:
- ❖ Father, I come to you in Jesus name to ask for Your forgiveness in my wrong choice of spouse.
- ❖ Father, please forgive me for deliberately going against Your will in my undertakings.
- ❖ Lord, I am deep in this relationship that is draining so much out of me, please grant me the wisdom and courage to know what to do and to do just that.
- ❖ Father please help me to find favour and forgiveness with my loved ones whom I have offended by my choice of spouse.
- ❖ Lord, in Your mercy, please give me the grace and humility to seek for godly counsel.
- ❖ Lord, please help me to walk out of this relationship alive in Jesus' name.
- ❖ Father, please grant me Your grace for a new

and better future in Jesus' name I pray with thanksgiving [Amen].

You may also wish to talk to professional Christian counsellors from any of the following organizations:
- www.eCounseling.com
  Tel. Number: 1-866-268-6735
- Full Gospel Business Men's International Fellowship: www.fgbmfi.org,
  Tel. Number: +1 949 461 0100
- www.marriagetoday.com/resources/.
- www.theshepherdsministries.org
- www.totalwoman

You can also read articles from:
- www.wisegeek.com/why-do-women-return-to- abusive-relationships.html
- www.bwss.org/home/contact-bwss/

CHAPTER 4

IN-LAWS

"For from henceforth there shall be five in one house divided, three against two, and two against three. The father shall be divided against the son, and the son against the father; the mother against the daughter, and the daughter against the mother; the mother in law against her daughter in law, and the daughter in law against her mother in law."
[Luke 12:52-53 (KJV)]

According to a popular African adage, it is better to marry a bad wife than to have a bad in-law. This is understandable because in traditional African culture, the extended family system of communal living and relationships is highly celebrated.

In-laws are extended family members of a couple from either side and under normal circumstances, their goal should be to nourish and support a couple in every way that would ensure the success of their marriage and relationship. Unfortunately this is not the case in a number of instances; more so, in the African setting where the system of communal living invites unnecessary intrusions and tends to be sometimes over stretched. But what do you do when an in-law begins to act like an outlaw? Let's look at an example in the Bible.

In a rage of jealousy and an attempt to destroy David, King

IN-LAWS

Saul tactically lured him to marry one of his daughters that he might have an easy opportunity to kill him. David felt his becoming the king's in-law was a daunting proposition given his humble background. However after several persuasions, he gave in to pressure and accepted Michal as wife.

Whilst still married to Michal, King Saul sought to kill David by trying to pin him to the wall with his spear. When that failed, on another occasion, King Saul sent for David from his marital home with the intention to kill him, an action which had he succeeded, would have made Michal, his daughter, a widow at an early age.

> *"In marriage, our primary responsibility is to protect and encourage our spouse. Where they are weak, God has equipped you and I to be strong so we should help our spouse unreservedly. We need to protect our spouses from 'killers' like food, friends, hobbies, dangerous family members, work mates, bosses, managers etc. Our spouse's success or failure is ours as well. Our assignment as a spouse includes protecting our children and others in our households."* [1]

One should not be surprised if some of the people especially in-laws who initially supported your wedding turn and start to do things that can harm or damage the marriage or turn to be the worst enemies of the marriage. What can one do with such people?

Culled from 'To the Bride with Love' by ©Oluwakemi Ola –Ojo 2010
ISBN: 978-0-9557898-4-7

- Love them and care for them unconditionally.
- Pray for them.
- Be extra careful and vigilant around such people.
- Do not hold the sins of your in-laws against your spouse for he or she may not be supportive of the aggravations they are giving you.
- Love your spouse and try to be in unity with them irrespective of the bad experience you have from your in-laws.
- Never compete with your in-laws in words, deeds or actions as marriage is not a game or race.

Are you having a difficult time with your in-laws? Then you may want to say these prayers:

Prayer points:
- ❖ Lord, please deliver me from every wicked in-law.
- ❖ Lord, please show me how to love and pray for my wicked, uncaring or un- thoughtful in-law(s).
- ❖ Lord, may I not fall into any deadly traps set by my in-law(s).
- ❖ Father, please deliver me from every spear or arrow that has been or is being thrown at me by my in-law(s).
- ❖ Lord, just as David outlived wicked King Saul, please Lord, protect and preserve my life so that I may outlive all my wicked in-laws in Jesus' name.

IN-LAWS

- ❖ Lord, please grant me the wisdom on how to manage my relationship with my spouse such that intruding and wicked in-laws will not destroy our relationship and lives in Jesus name.
- ❖ Father, please grant me Your favour and that of all people and teach me on how to live at peace with people in Jesus' name I pray with thanksgiving.

CHAPTER 5

COLLEAGUES

"Then this Daniel was preferred above the presidents and princes, because an excellent spirit was in him; and the king thought to set him over the whole realm. Then the presidents and princes sought to find occasion against Daniel concerning the kingdom; but they could find none occasion nor fault; forasmuch as he was faithful, neither was there any error or fault found in him. Then said these men, We shall not find any occasion against this Daniel, except we find it against him concerning the law of his God.
[Daniel 6:3-5 (KJV)]

For many people, the time spent at work is limited to their working hours which could range from, 30 to 40 hours a week on the average. For a few others, the time spent at work could go beyond this figure, especially at executive levels where policy decisions are made. Either way, the remaining hours of the week is spent by people as they choose outside of work. Even though the time spent in the workplace is limited, those few weekly hours could feel like years of torture when colleagues gang up against a person. Let's examine a few of such people.

COLLEAGUES

Daniel:
Daniel and his friends were among the people that had been taken into exile in Babylon during the time of King Jehoiakim of Judah. He with a few of his friends were among those chosen by the King to be fed and trained in all the ways of the Babylonians. They were to be in the king's service upon graduation from their training. The king personally conducted the final examinations and found Daniel and his friends to be ten times better than indigenes who were magicians and astrologers in matters of wisdom and understanding. The king promoted Daniel to become the president over 120 governors *[Daniel 1:1-21, 2:31-49]*. Daniel's excellent spirit and faultless performance at work made him to become the target of some of his colleagues, who ganged up against him and plotted to have him killed. They devised a plan to have the king kill him by getting him thrown into the lion's den. The Lord rescued Daniel from the lion's den by a miraculous act in which the lions failed to devour him. When the king discovered Daniel's unprecedented deliverance by God, he ordered that those who plotted against him, together with their entire families, be thrown into the lion's den. The lions who had gone without food overnight suddenly found their appetites restored and immediately devoured the enemies and their families. Consequently, a new decree which favoured Daniel was set in place by the king *[Daniel 6:1-28]*.

We must let the quality and quantity of our work speak

for us among colleagues. We must keep focused on God and our God-given assignment. When we do this, God will always come through for you and me.

Shadrach, Messach and Abednego
[Daniel 3: 1- 4:3].
These talented, hardworking young men found themselves appearing before the king because of their faith in Jehovah. Their colleagues had set them up for total destruction. Their refusal to bow to the king's image brought the king's wrath and he asked that the fiery furnace be heated seven times more. The men who threw the three Hebrew youths into the fiery furnace were instantaneously killed by the heat of the fire yet the three Hebrew youths escaped unscathed; not even their clothes smelt of fire! The fire could only cut the ropes they were bound with and they walked about of the fire with God joining them as the fourth person. Don't be surprised as a child of God if and when your colleagues turn themselves into an adversary. Keep your faith, continue to work as one serving God, not succumbing to the enemies' threats, working above board i.e. becoming exceptionally excellent in what you do, stand your ground against every ungodly opposition and watch God dramatically deliver you and destroy your enemies.

Judas Iscariot
Among the many people that followed Jesus Christ

COLLEAGUES

during His earthly ministry was Judas Iscariot, chosen by Jesus Himself to be among his twelve disciples. In addition, Judas Iscariot was also chosen to be the treasurer for the group. Both positions were that of trust and therefore enviable. Judas Iscariot was with the disciples learning at the Master's feet and getting a deeper insight and understanding of the kingdom of God whilst getting a firsthand education on experience, yet he chose to betray Jesus Christ at a cost of thirty pieces of silver! Whilst he lived to regret his decision to betray an innocent man, the evil had been done and could not be undone.

Have you ever helped someone to get a position in your establishment and the same person turns completely against you once they complete their probation? Have you helped someone set up a similar business to yours and as their own kind gesture, taken over all your major clients? Have you been betrayed and lied against to the extent that you have lost precious relationships, business, trust, etc. or ended up being jailed for an offence that you did not commit? I would like to encourage you to take the situation to the All-knowing, seeing, hearing and feeling God. Let Him fight your battles for you and deliver you. Whatever loss arises from such betrayal, we must thank God for He is able to make it better for you as He is able to turn all your losses to profits and promotion.

When I was about age seventeen years old, I was betrayed

by our class captain in the Midwifery School. My betrayer was a daughter to one of my Mum's colleagues at work. I had not done anything wrong or failed any examination. It was that I had gone to take counsel against a particular oncoming evil decision that would affect my ongoing study. Unknown to me, my betrayer had been planted by the authority to pretend to support me but monitor my movement and decision. Her betrayal invariably cost me my life ambition of becoming a midwife. I lost an academic year and changed careers. It was a very painful, devastating but God-approved experience. Today as I look back and write, my testimony can be summed up as written by Paul in *Romans 8:28, "For we know that God makes all things work together for good to those who love God and are called according to His purpose."*

Working in an unconducive atmosphere could be very stressful and challenging but God is able to deliver you and may I suggest that you:

- Get your relationship right with God always.
- Be the best on your job i.e. Do your work with excellence.
- Be nice to your colleague's in spite of their ganging up.
- Do not repay evil with evil.
- Trust God to deliver you and pray.

Should you have been a victim of colleague's enmity then you may wish to pray along these lines:

COLLEAGUES

Prayer Points:
- Lord, please grant me the courage and wisdom to be able to perform my duties in my secular job above board.
- In every crisis, open my eyes to see the available and corresponding opportunities. Also help me to use such to my advantage in Jesus' name.
- Father, please expose every gang-up of enemies at my place of work.
- Lord, may my enemies be destroyed by the wicked plans they have devised for me.
- Father, please grant me the ability to forgive all my enemies in Jesus' name.
- God, please grant me divine favours with all the people that matter in my chosen career.
- In spite of all the oppositions, may my life witness and mirror your love to all I come in contact with at work.
- Lord, please promote me at work and please bless all the works of my hand in Jesus Christ name have I prayed and with thanksgiving. Amen.[2]

---

[1] A good book to read: '10 commandments at work' by T.D. Jakes

CHAPTER 6

BOSSES, MANAGERS OR EMPLOYERS

"And they found an Egyptian in the field, and brought him to David, and gave him bread, and he did eat; and they made him drink water; And they gave him a piece of a cake of figs, and two clusters of raisins: and when he had eaten, his spirit came again to him: for he had eaten no bread, nor drunk any water, three days and three nights. And David said unto him, To whom belongest thou? and whence art thou? And he said, I am a young man of Egypt, servant to an Amalekite; and my master left me, because three days agone I fell sick."
[1 Samuel 30:11-13 (KJV)]

An enterprise or company is only as strong as their staff. The best resource an organization has is its staff and not the gadgets or facilities. What do you do when you are using all your time, talent and skills and yet your boss or employer is trying to kill you? Let us examine a few examples in the Bible of people who had such experiences.

Saul and David
David's first encounter with King Saul was when he visited him and his brothers on the battle field. Though not of age to be part of King's Saul army, he decided to risk his life to defend the name of the Lord that was at stake.

His victory over Goliath led to King Saul to enquire about his background *[1 Samuel 17: 55-57]*. The women's song about that victory caused King Saul to become jealous of David. The consequence of that was God taking away His Spirit from King Saul and replacing it with a tormenting spirit *[1 Samuel 18: 5-10]*. To cure King Saul, his advisors suggested that David be employed to minister to him in music. King Saul sent to Jesse for David to be released for his service. Even though David served King Saul with the best of his skills, talents, time and life, yet on many occasions King Saul tried to pin him to the wall with the spear *[1 Samuel 18:10-11, 19:9-10]* and when that failed, King Saul sent him on dangerous errands and wars with the hope of getting him killed *[1 Samuel 18: 25]* and when that did not work, King Saul sent for David from his home so as to kill him *[1 Samuel 19:11–17]*. Finally when all these failed, he pursued David all around so as to kill him *[1 Samuel 23-24:22]* though David was one of his in-laws!

If you experience such harassment and pursuit like David, then do what he did. He put his trust and faith in God, the creator of heaven and earth, absolutely. He served King Saul faithfully and diligently. He refused to kill King Saul when he had the opportunity *[1 Samuel 24:1-11]*, he protected any that was harassed with their families and he fed the hungry *[1 Samuel 30]*.

King David killed Uriah the Hittite
After many years of pursuit by King Saul, King Saul and

his son Jonathan were both killed at war. Then David was crowned as King first in Judah and later over the whole nation of Israel *[2 Samuel 2:1-11, 5:1-5]*. He continued going out to war with his troops until his men requested him to stay at home.

In his boredom, he took a walk on his balcony and saw beautiful Bathsheba. In his lust and momentary disconnection from God, he took another man's wife, slept with her and got her pregnant. When he learnt of his growing seed in Bathsheba, he tried covering up by inviting Uriah – Bathsheba's husband – to return from the battlefield in order to lure him to sleep with Bathsheba. When his trick failed, he wrote a letter for Uriah to be killed. That worked and he thought all was over *[2 Samuel 11:1-27]*.

How many bosses have transferred their staff out of town far away from their home base so that they may have an illicit affair with their spouses? How many have insisted on their sleeping with their workers' wives/ husbands before giving them or their spouses their rightful entitlements? How many bosses and managers have given verbal or written references that literally terminated the career of their vulnerable subordinates who had trusted them?

Uriah the Hittite, the sharp shooter, the defender of God's ark and his King died prematurely because of King David's illicit affair with his beautiful wife.

King Nebuchadnezzar

King Nebuchadnezzar of Babylon had the fiery furnace heated up seven times to kill Shadrach, Meshach and Abednego who were serving in his court. Their offence was that the three Hebrew men refused to bow down and worship his golden image. These three men up till the time the golden image was erected were serving as governors in King Nebuchadnezzar's government. God came to their rescue because they had declared their allegiance only to the Master, Creator and Sustainer of same *[Daniel 3: 1- 4:3]*.

Friend for as long as we do not become weary doing good things then God will show up. Our God is the Master of the universe and all that has ever been created. In many work places today, while it is fashionable to discuss political issues, football etc., it is unpopular and frowned at once a child of God declares his/her relationship with thier Maker. That is not to say we should not continue to express our faith in Jesus Christ.

Should your manager or boss be out for your job or life in spite your giving your job the best then you may wish to pray along these lines:

Prayer Points:
- ❖ Lord, please grant me Your divine protection from my boss who is after my life and job.
- ❖ Lord, in Your mercy grant me the grace and wisdom to do my work diligently in spite of all the opposition at my place work.

THE ENEMY WITHIN

- ❖ Father, in You alone have I put my trust, let me not be ashamed and let not my enemies triumph over me.
- ❖ Lord, protect me from friends, family members and associates who might want to cooperate with my enemies against me in my absence.
- ❖ Father, I need to work and earn a decent living, please protect me from every manager or boss who might want to terminate my life, career and relationship with my spouse or children prematurely.
- ❖ As I go about my daily tasks, Lord help me to be focused on You and what You can achieve through me in spite of all the oppositions.
- ❖ Lord, please terminate the contract of any manager or boss whose assignment from the devil is against Your will for my life in Jesus' name I pray and with thanksgiving. Amen

CHAPTER 7

NEIGHBOURS

"And the people shall be oppressed, every one by another, and every one by his neighbour: ..."
[Isaiah 3:5 (KJV)]

Many people, tenants or home owners, hardly have a choice as to who their neighbour is, whether in their home or work environment. There are different kinds of neighbours – neutral neighbours, good neighbours and there are 'neighbours from hell', as described in a popular United Kingdom television programme.

Again, let us consider two of such from the Bible:

Naboth and King Ahab
[1Kings 21:1-27]
Ideally, anybody would like to be a neighbour to a reigning king and the reason for this is not far fetched. This is because there are many benefits one could gain from being a king's neighbour. Such would include extra protection from the kings' guards, proximity to high profile visitors passing by, the king's generosity, etc. however, for Naboth's family, being neighbour to a rich ruler and king was to their detriment.

Naboth a poor man, was a neighbour to King Ahab. All he had as an inheritance from his forefathers included a well-groomed vegetable garden which unfortunately had caught the eyes of the king. King Ahab wanted to buy it off Naboth but Nahobth was unwilling to sell it as it was his inheritance and by cultural belief, was meant to remain in the family forever. Jezebel, the queen heard about the king's unmet desire and she quickly organized Naboth's murder. Thereafter, the vineyard was automatically repossessed by the wicked royal family.

How many wives, helpers, valuable properties, lands and staff have been more or less forcefully lured and taken over by richer neighbours? They perpetrate their wicked acts often thinking they are above the law of the land, and cannot be challenged by the poor or feeble person(s) they have just robbed or killed. However, they are far from the truth for there is a King above who sees all, knows all and cannot be cajoled or bribed. And He who has promised to defend and avenge those who take advantage of the poor, widow or feeble ones *[Exodus 23:6, Leviticus 25:17, Proverbs 22:16, 22, Deuteronomy 23:16, Zechariah 7:10, Malachi 3:5].*

The Two Prostitutes
[1Kings 3:16-27]
Two prostitutes lived in the same house doing the same job and delivered babies around the same time. One night, one of them carelessly slept on her baby, killing

him in the process. Realizing what had happened, she quickly and quietly exchanged the dead baby with her neighbour's living baby. In the morning the other prostitute discovered what had happened and both went to seek the counsel of King Solomon. The careless prostitute was quite happy to have half of the dead child and half of the living child but not the mother of the living child.

A careless and wicked neighbour will be comfortable with you suffering loss out of their carelessness. The advise will be for each one of us to be prayerful, careful and very vigilant should we have a careless neighbour lest the bill for their carelessness lands on our table.

Prayer Points:
- ❖ Father, in Your mercy deliver me from wicked and harmful neighbours in Jesus' name.
- ❖ Lord, please protect my family, land and properties from my neighbour who might want to destroy me because of my lawful inheritance.
- ❖ Father, may every counsel of any and every oppressive neighbour be cancelled in the name of Jesus Christ.
- ❖ Lord, I refuse any and every neighbour trading the life of my living, vibrant, anointed spouse, children or property for their 'dead' ones in Jesus' name.
- ❖ Lord, please build a hedge of protection and a wall of fire around me and all that is mine in Jesus' name.

THE ENEMY WITHIN

- ❖ I reject every swapping of my family's great destiny with any other neighbour's dead destiny in Jesus' name.
- ❖ Father, please help that I am not a neighbour from hell or have a neighbour from hell in Jesus name I have prayed with thanksgiving. Amen

CHAPTER 8

WICKED LEADERS

"And the king answered the people roughly, and forsook the old men's counsel that they gave him; And spake to them after the counsel of the young men, saying, My father made your yoke heavy, and I will add to your yoke: my father also chastised you with whips, but I will chastise you with scorpions."
[1 Kings 12:13-14 (KJV)]

Herod and Pharaoh

Is it not strange that leaders who are meant to provide care and support to their subjects could sometimes be agents of mass destruction to them? Let's look at some scenarios in the Bible.

Pharaoh

Many years after the death of Joseph, another king arose that did not know Joseph nor what he had done for the kingdom of Egypt [Exodus 1:8]. He saw the seeds of Joseph, a one-time deliverer of Egypt as a threat to his nation. In his unfounded fear, he embarked on a mission of mass destruction of an innocent and helpless nation whose forefathers had come to bring solution to the famine that could have wiped out the whole nation of Egypt, indeed the whole world [Genesis 41:53-57]. This new Pharaoh looked for all the ways of limiting the growth and comfort of the Jews. He set a new decree to kill all newly born boys to the Jewish families so as to weaken the strength and morale of Israel as a nation. When that did not work, he enslaved the entire nation, making them build pyramids, and doing many menial jobs with the hope of breaking their spirit and soul *[Exodus 1:8-14]*.

When invariably Moses came to rescue God's people, Pharaoh refused to let the people go to worship and serve their God in spite of the various plagues visited on the nation by God, until God killed every first born of man and animal in one night! The Israelites were reluctantly allowed to leave but soon after, Pharaoh and the best of his military power pursued them *[Exodus 14:1-31]*.

Are there not bosses and jobs that will do anything to prevent you and I from worshipping and serving our God? How many do overtime especially on worship days because of the double or time and a half payment? The Bible says we are not to neglect the fellowship of one another *[Hebrews 10:25]*.

King Herod
The star announced to the wise men, the birth of a king, one who was to be recognized, celebrated and appreciated. Herod, the reigning king in Judea was informed by the visiting wise men of the birth of a new born baby King in his kingdom. That was very frightening

and disturbing for King Herod but he pretended to be interested in finding this unknown baby king so that he could also go and worship him. He therefore instructed the wise men to go and search for the baby king and bring back word to him of his whereabouts. But when the wise men did not return as promised, he issued a decree to kill every boy under the age of two years old. For just one baby that he was looking for, he went on a rampage, totally wiping out his innocent, helpless subjects.

The same thing happened with the baby Moses when the Pharaoh gave instructions for every male child born to a Hebrew to be killed because he wanted to prevent the Hebrews from growing in number. In both cases, God miraculously spared the lives of the ones both kings were looking for while their male age mates died [Matthew 1:18-2:18, Exodus 1:15- 2:10].

Every parent should pray for divine protection for their children especially from people who may have an ulterior motive in visiting or giving gifts to them or the baby.

Mrs. Potiphar
Although married to an influential officer of Pharaoh, a highly placed and powerful man, a captain of Pharaoh's guard and indeed, a man of affluence and influence, yet Pharaoh's wife was not satisfied.

For whatever reasons, she pursued Joseph, her husband's servant, desperately, in a bid to sleep with him. When Joseph refused to give in and ran away she lied against him and got him into the maximum security prison *[Genesis 39:7-20]*. It is common to find bosses, men and women alike, who pressurize their employees into having illicit sexual affairs with them for the return of one favour or the other or sometimes just out of sheer blackmail. However, it has been discovered time and time again that getting involved in such relationships does not guarantee any job or position in the long run and sometimes even fail to materialize at all! Should you be in that situation, may I encourage you to do what Joseph did, run for your life, future and destiny lest you lose God's plan and will for your life.

There is no permanent job or job location for life. Most professionals move around within their industry. It is generally allowed and often times such movements allows us to broaden our base, experience, professional and social network. So don't be glued to a location for life especially when your life or integrity is being compromised.

You need a job and an income but not at the expense of your life, faith, health and destiny. A wise person knows when it is best to quit a job and run for their life like Joseph. It is a sign of strength not weakness.

Should any of your bosses be out for your job or life in spite of your giving your job the best then prayerfully seek godly counsel and you may wish to pray along these lines:

Prayer Points:
- ❖ Lord, give us leaders who will fear You and live within Your love and commandments.
- ❖ Lord, please help that my ways may please You always so that all my enemies will be at peace with me.
- ❖ Lord, confuse all the powers that are after my life and job in Jesus' name.
- ❖ Jehovah, please protect me as I do my work daily.
- ❖ Father, please help me not to compromise on my time of fellowship with You and other believers.
- ❖ Lord, please help me not to succumb to any ungodly, sexual, verbal and non - verbal, physical, emotional or financial harassment at work in Jesus' name.
- ❖ Lord, help me to keep focused on Your plans and destiny for me in Jesus' name. Amen

CHAPTER 9

SICKNESS AND POVERTY

The rich man's wealth is his strong city:
the destruction of the poor is their poverty.
[Proverbs 10:15 (KJV)]

In our introduction to this book, we defined the word enemy as *"an unfriendly opponent who hates or seeks to harm somebody or something. It can also be a person or group especially military force that fights against another in combat or battle or a hostile nation or power. It can also be something that harms or opposes something else. It is an adversary or foe or rival."*

However, in this chapter, we would like to expand the definition to include "anyone or anything that:
- Promotes the weakening or pollution of our soul, body or spirit.
- Rubbishes, demeans or devalues our calling or anointing.
- Refuses to acknowledge God or His calling over or anointing in our lives.
- Fuels our physical, financial, emotional, psychological or spiritual weaknesses.
- Works against our strength.
- Cannot or does not speak well about us or whatever matters to us.

- Does not value our existence or feels threatened by same."

In view of this expanded definition, we would like to consider the following conditions as enemies within.

Sicknesses and diseases
These conditions either bring discomfort, limitations and pain. Every disease is an enemy trying to rub one of a good life, a good health and often wanting to distract the sick from achieving their purpose in life. Someone once said disease means dis- ease! It is not the wish of God for us to be ill. God equally does not punish us with sickness. While many diseases are a direct result of our wrong choices and lifestyles, some diseases are just hereditary, that is, they are passed down from our ancestors, directly from our parents genetically, without our permission or their intentions.

Some diseases are there for reasons that only God knows why - He permits it like in the case of the man born blind but whatever the disease, we do have a name that is above the disease and 'at the mention of the name of Jesus, every knee (including that of the disease) shall bow down' *[Philippians. 2: 9-11]*.

Personally, I believe that diseases, sicknesses, and demonic oppressions have ears to hear God's command and rebuke. Most, if not all the healings in the Bible were achieved through the spoken words of a prophet, apostle or Jesus Christ.

To overcome any disease, let us consider the following points (not in any particular order):

- Identify the name of the disease.
- If you can, find out the cause of the disease – is it due to a lifestyle or habit that can be reversed or corrected? Or is it congenital?
- Is it due to a previous accident or injury e.g. Mephibosheth became lame due to a spinal injury following a fall when he was young *[2 Samuel 4:4]*.
- Give your life to Jesus Christ for we need to have a relationship with Him in order for Him to be able to help us fight our battles. He has a name greater than any affliction or disease.
- We need to serve and obey Him. *"And ye shall serve Jehovah your God, and he will bless thy bread, and thy water; and I will take sickness away from the midst of thee. There shall none cast her young, nor be barren, in thy land: the number of thy days I will fulfill" [Exodus 23:25-26]*.
- Meditate on healing scriptures such as *"By His stripes we are healed" [1 Peter 2:24], Exodus 15:26 says "If thou wilt diligently hearken to the voice of the Lord thy God, and wilt do that which is right in his sight, and wilt give ear to his commandments, and keep all his statutes, I will put none of these diseases upon thee, which I have brought upon the Egyptians: for I [am] the LORD that healeth thee" [Psalms 118:17]*.
- You will need to resist the devil in the name and power of the Lord. James 4:7 says, "Submit

SICKNESS AND POVERTY

yourselves therefore to God. Resist the devil, and he will flee from you."

- Confess the scriptures every day, as often as possible, at least as often as you take the medication for the disease. Confess your healing before you see the physical manifestation for the Bible says "faith comes by hearing and hearing by the word of God" [Romans 10:17]. What we receive in our spirit will be manifested according to the word and will of God for you and I in Jesus' name.
- What about using the prescribed medication? To this, I would say please keep using the prescribed drugs until you receive the physical manifestation of your healing.

Prayer points:
- ❖ Confess any sins to God in repentance and ask Him for His forgiveness.
- ❖ Father, in any way that my life style and choices have caused this sickness (name the sickness), I ask for Your pardon and forgiveness in Jesus' name. Please help me from now to depend on Your Holy Spirit for the ability to overcome any bad life style or choice that is negatively affecting my health in Jesus' name.
- ❖ Lord, Your word says that Jesus has come to give me life and life in abundance therefore I receive my full healing and abundant life in Jesus' name.
- ❖ You foul spirit of (name the disease or the

sickness), the Lord Jesus rebuke you in His name and by His stripes I am healed.
- *(Name the disease)*, you are a weapon fashioned against me but you and your activities shall not prosper in my body as my body is the temple of the Lord and you disease is not permitted to defile it in Jesus' name.
- I resist in the name of Jesus every seed and manifestation of (name the disease or sickness) in my body and family in Jesus' name.
- Father, please visit the source of my sickness and disease and pour Your healing salt into it so that from now on, Your own life of good health will begin to flow out of me in Jesus name *[See 2kings 2: 19-22]*.

Poverty

The Bible says in Deuteronomy 15:11, *"For the poor will never cease out of the land and Jesus also said that there will always be some poor people in the land [Matthew 26:11 and John 12:8].* In my opinion, it is better to be rich than poor. Poverty is a terrible disease and enemy. It robs anyone of the ability to progress. It limits the individual. Poverty causes hunger and malnutrition, various sicknesses and diseases which if it persists and is untreated, kills. The poor often have to depend on the generosity of the rich, subject to handouts, pass downs, all sorts of abuse and misuse, sometimes to the detriment of their lives, health and future. They may have to sell their property, inheritance or themselves at such a low price, to a wrong cause, or a wrong person etc. *[Amos 8:6, Proverbs 22:7]*. A poor person's idea is often ignored, rejected and may never see the light of the day and, if care is not taken, it goes unrewarded *[Ecclesiastes 9:15-16]*. A poor person may be hated by other family members and may lose their friends *[Proverbs 19:7]*.

Unfortunately, some people are born into poverty, while for some, their lifestyle and choices leave them poor *[Proverbs 21:7]*. The prodigal son in *Luke 15: 11-24* started off from home very wealthy with his own inheritance but with his choice of friends and lifestyle abroad, he ended up being very poor, without the guarantee of a good meal per day. God at creation put more than enough resources in the world but as it was at the time of Adam and the Israelites, we each have to go and find the wealth.

Dr. Nasir Sidiqui, during a programme on Trinity Broadcasting Network on November 26, 2009, mentioned that very often, people end up poor because of **P**assing **O**ver **O**pportunities **R**epeatedly.

How to overcome poverty *(not in any particular order)*
- Acknowledge the poverty whether it is physical, financial, spiritual, emotional, etc.
- Give your life to Jesus if you have not done that before [John 3:16]. Luke 4:18 says *"The Spirit of the Lord is upon me, because He anointed me to preach good tidings to the poor: He hath sent me to proclaim release to the captives, And recovering*

of sight to the blind, to set at liberty them that are bruised.
- There is an anointing that is more than enough to break the yoke of poverty, release the poor, bring recovery and set one free in Jesus Christ."
- Identify the source of your poverty e.g. If you were born into a poor family could it be due to passing over opportunities repeatedly? Is it as a result of ignorance of the decision makers in your family, is it due to famine, lack of rain or natural disasters? Or is it due to wrong lifestyle or habits or wrong associates or wrong decision(s)?
- You cannot be lazy and hope to get out of poverty. Hard work does not kill, it strengthens and empowers one *[Proverbs 6:6,9; 13:4; 20:4; 26: 16].*
- If you were born into a poor family, please don't despise your parents or siblings but take it as perhaps you are meant to be the family deliverer and with God's help and hard work, poverty will be a thing of the past in Jesus' name. Joseph of old was and so can you be too.
- Seek the counsel and wisdom of God in prayers and study of His words. You may wish to meditate on passages like *[Psalms 9:12,18, 10:12, 12:5, 34:6, 35:10, 40,17, 69:29, 70:5, 72: 4,12-13, 74:19,21].*
- Prayerfully identify your God-given talent or skill or resource. For the poor widow it was her bottle of oil *[1Kings 4:1-7].* Yours might be your voice, effective writing or good communicating abilities, sewing or dress making, cooking,

computer skills, praying, teaching, a pond in your compound, fertile farm land, ability to repair objects and articles, interpretation of dreams, nursing etc.
- Do not despise your God-given talent or skill or resource or allow anyone to do so. Speak prayerfully and positively about them. God gives you and I the seed in form of our talent, skill, and resource but it is as we sow or use them that we get blessed *[Matthew 25:14-30].*
- Seek godly and wise counsel on how to make use of your talent and resource to the maximum.
- To get out of poverty using your God-given talent, skill or resource may not be an easy task. There will be oppositions, attacks, challenges and all manners of obstacles on your journey but you must be determined and focused on God to help you every step of the way *[See Joseph in Genesis 39:2-6, 20-22].*
- Do not compromise on your integrity or faith on your way to success as there will be multiple temptations and seemingly 'short-cuts'.
- Learn to share and give to others from what you have and can afford on your way out of poverty. The Bible says in *Luke 6:38, "Give, and it shall be given unto you; good measure, pressed down, and shaken together, and running over, shall men give into your bosom. For with the same measure that ye mete with it shall be measured to you again."*
- For anyone who has given their life to Jesus

Christ, tithing from your resources and income is not an option but a good way out of poverty. If you have nothing, then give a tithe of your time in praying, sharing the gospel and helping others.

Prayer points:
- Father, in the name of Jesus, I confess every bad habit or wrong lifestyle or choices that has brought me into poverty in Jesus' name.
- Lord, in Your name I come against every ancestral curse or yoke of poverty in my family. I denounce the spirit of poverty and confess that my inheritance as a child of God is wealth and not poverty.
- Lord, I ask for Your pardon for every missed opportunity to success and progress in life and ask that in Your mercy You will bring other opportunities for breakthrough in Jesus name. Please Lord, help me to be more sensitive to the leading of the Holy Spirit as from now in Jesus name. Help me to respond to His prompting too.
- Father, I am grateful to You for the following talents and skills that I have (mention them).
- Lord, I bring these talents and skills to you and ask for an outpouring of Your Holy Spirit and Your divine wisdom on how to enhance and use them for Your glory and blessings of mankind.
- In every way that I have compromised and not paid my tithe as a child of God, I come confessing and ask for Your mercy and help to pay my tithe and give my offerings as from now on in Jesus name.

SICKNESS AND POVERTY

- ❖ With the skills and talents that I have been given, please Lord, help me to focus on how best to use them, not to be lazy or distracted and please line my part in life with destiny helpers that You have ordained for me in Jesus' name. Lord I choose to be rich rather than poor, healthy spiritually, physically, materially, financially, emotionally and all round, rather than being sick, from now in Jesus' name. Amen

CHAPTER 10

SELF

"I can of mine own self do nothing: as I hear, I judge: and my judgment is just; because I seek not mine own will, but the will of the Father which hath sent me."
[John 5:30 (KJV)]

The greatest enemy of a man is self. The Bible says a house that is divided against itself cannot stand. Nobody knows you and I like we do. Normally one should not be working against oneself. Unfortunately, it is not uncommon to find people who indulge in actions and activities that work against themselves. Now let's see some factors that could turn a person to being their own enemy, whether consciously or otherwise:

Wrong or Evil Associates
Proverbs 1:10 says *"my son if sinners entice you, do not consent".* Wrong or evil association or acting on wrong advice no matter who gives it may make one become their own enemy. Bad association corrupts good morals. Amnon, one of King David's sons followed through an evil associate's advice that led to his ultimate death. Jonadab his cunning cousin instead of giving Amnon a godly advice, gave him a wicked advice. Many people will end up in hell because of their evil associates and many more are in prison today as a result of their evil companions *[2 Samuel 13]*.

Many have truncated their lives, destiny and dreams because of the wrong friends and relationships they kept. Surrounding one's self with goalless, visionless, dreamless people and things is as dangerous as toying with dangerous weapons. An English adage says, 'show me your friend and I will tell you who you are.' A wrong association will leave anyone visionless, ineffective and imprisoned. Samson's association with Delilah invariable cost him his God-given strength and anointing, his eyes, his vision and his mission. He was imprisoned and made to grind food for his enemies, dance for his enemies before their gods and eventually his destiny was terminated. In his choice was his end.

Bad Habits/Attitudes

The Bible says our bodies are the temple of God. Bad habits such as smoking, over or under eating, or eating the wrong foods and snacks can damage our health. Medically speaking, it now a known fact that passive or active smoking is dangerous to anybody's health. It has been said that in the United Kingdom one can get a new car for the cost of smoking over a period of 3-5years. Smoking pregnant women are more prone to bleeding in early pregnancy and having small babies. In the same way that indulgencies such as fornication or adultery excessive consumption of alcohol or spirits, stealing like the thief on the cross, contaminates our bodies and soul and they may either cause untimely death or diseases - curable and incurable, loss of work, respect or dignity.

Many have eaten their ways into unhealthy, preventable and detrimental medical conditions. Our bodies are the temples of God therefore we ought to be careful what food, thought, habit or lifestyles that goes into it. *2 Corinthians 6:12* tells us that *"all things are lawful for me but not all things are helpful, all things are lawful for me but I shall not be enslaved by anything."* It was for freedom that Christ has set us free no longer to be subject to the yoke of slavery. Wrong choices and bad lifestyles are major contributions to many damaging health and wealth conditions.

The Bible enjoins us to have a healthy attitude to ourselves and others. Many who have allowed their bodies to rule them negatively have had themselves to blame. Our bodies are the temples of God therefore we ought to be careful what food we eat and the habit we indulge in. The mouth that says the wrong things or overfeeds may leave its owner either in jail for saying the wrong things or in the hospital for obesity or diabetes. Those who have allowed their hands to participate in evil or legs to take them to ungodly places including indulgence in pornography are now having to deal with guilt and fear whilst others who have lusted after other people's spouse have lost their own marriage, relationship or caught one of the sexually transmitted disease curable or incurable.

Bad attitudes such as bad temper, uncontrolled anger or unforgiveness can cause diseases including headaches, high blood pressure etc. What has unforgiveness cost you and what is it costing you even now? Is it worth the price you pay in losing your good health and being tormented by an evil spirit?

While the Bible says we must be angry but not sin, uncontrolled anger torments the person who is harbouring such, makes the person build a mountain out of a molehill and if care is not taken leads to self or other people's destructive plans. A wise man once said if you find yourself not being loved by others, check your character. The older brother in the story of the prodigal son locked himself out of the restoration and celebration party due to anger and wrong attitude. We must avoid going to bed especially at night with any form of anger lest we expose ourselves to heart attacks or demonic oppression.

Anyone with an unforgiving spirit really does not love themselves. *Matthew 6:12* says *"forgive us our sins as we forgive others that sin against us"*. We all need God's mercy and forgiveness. Not forgiving others disqualifies us from receiving pardon from our Maker. Unforgiveness releases toxin and pollution into our spirit and soul which invariably may harm our bodies. If God should mark iniquity not one of us can stand. Forgiveness gives us room to receive God's mercy.

Difficult as it may be, we must not allow ourselves to be dragged and remain in any bad attitude to God, ourselves and others.

Ingratitude

There is an African adage that says that if a child says thank you for yesterday's gift they will get more. Ten lepers approached Jesus Christ for healing and all the ten received their healing but only one came back to say thank you, he was the only one that was made whole. There is nothing that we have in life that was not given to us beginning from our lives, breath, water, food etc. We ought to learn to return the thanks always to the Giver of life and Sustainer of same. Equally nobody, not even our God owes anybody anything. We need to be grateful when God or someone helps us and not take them or God for granted. Psalms 100 encourages us to enter His gates with thanksgiving in our hearts and enter His court with praise. Whoever helps us should be thanked from the depth of our hearts whether it is a child or adult, male or female etc. Ingratitude stops the flow of the blessings from the giver to us. No one likes being taken for granted. No one who is an ingrate can go far in life.

Self imposed limitations

Wrong confessions such as 'I cannot' limits what God can do through us and with us. For this, many of us Christians are guilty. We tend to look at our problems and magnify it way and above our God, the maker of heaven and earth. Ten out of the twelve spies said 'we are unable, we are like grasshoppers in our eyes.' That was their own assessment of themselves - not God's! Nor the enemies'! *[Numbers 13:26-33]*. They forgot who was with them and whose they were. The people made God angry and He said what they have spoken to His ears He has heard and that was to be the verdict [Numbers 14:28]. You and I must be mindful of our confessions even in difficult times. Ought we not to be careful about what we say? *[Proverbs 18:21* and *James 3:1-12].* The woman with the dead child said 'it is well', knowing fully-well that her only son was dead and lay on the prophet's bed and she continued to say 'it is well' until her confession became her possession. For your issues and mine we ought to realise and appreciate God, find the appropriate scripture and use it to buttress our belief. Equally, what and who we will listen to, who or what we watch or read will affect our thoughts. We need to pay a close attention to what is on our minds and thoughts as the Bible enjoins us to 'Keep your heart with all diligence; for out of it are the issues of life' *[Proverbs 4:23. KJV].*

For us as children of God, finding or identifying problems should energize us for that is our opportunity to be blessed. The world pays problem solvers so rather than confessing negatively and running away, we should in the wisdom of God find ways of providing solutions to the identified problems. If you and I can identify the problem then with the Lord's help we can find the solution to it.

Often times what comes out of our mouths is what has been in our thoughts and minds. For us to possess God's purpose for our lives, we must learn to align our thoughts with His will *[Matthew 15:18-19, 12:23, Proverbs 23, 19, Luke 6:45, Mark 7:21].*

Procrastination
This is the thief of time. How many of us have missed unique and rare opportunities because we procrastinated about what we should or should not do or where we should be or not. Even when God through the Holy Spirit is trying to remind us, how often do we ignore God's prompting and say later and eventually lose the opportunity. God in His love has more than enough provisions for our needs but we must avoid procrastination. One of the good attributes of Father Abraham was that he never procrastinated. As soon as he heard God he obeyed Him *[Genesis 12:1-4, 22:1-19].* A wise person said delayed or partial obedience is equivalent to disobedience *[1 Samuel 15:22].* In *2 Kings 4 :1-8*, the Shunamite woman immediately acted with regards to her dead child without waiting for the prophet's return from the prayer mountain or husband to return from the farm before she went to seek for help. Time was of essence and importance. One of the good characters of the prodigal son in Luke 15 was that he never procrastinated even when he had to return home, to eat the humble pie and face disgrace and relegation from being a son to becoming a servant.

No shame, disgrace, poverty, failure, displeasure and emptiness could keep him away from his father's unconditional love. Once we have prayed through we should avoid any form of delay and distraction. That which we have to do we must do and on time.

Laziness

In most things, God is always giving us opportunities. He is an equal opportunity provider most times. He gives the rich and the poor a single life each, He shines the sun on the rich and poor, old and young, male and female, He sends the rain on the wicked and just, fresh air to those who love or hate Him, He is an equal opportunity time provider with 24 hours per day for each, baby or toddler or adults, the lazy and the hard working. He gives each person at least a talent or gift. While workaholics find a reason for working many hours a day, the lazy people find a reason for not going to find a job or work on a job. They are full of excuses, complaints, murmurs and reasons why an idea, a proposal cannot work. If they at all work, they tend to want to do the barest minimum for their wages, some not even venturing to devise ways of working better and faster. They justify their laziness and blame everyone else but themselves. All they can see around them are problems and they do not want to find the cure or solutions to these problems. They limit themselves before trying and may try to blackmail their working or successful mates. God's blessings are often wrapped around instructions and problems. For example, David's obedience to visit his brothers on the battle field and the problem of who would fight Goliath the giant led to his becoming a national hero overnight.

Laziness is like a deadly disease making many to waste away with undiscovered, untapped and unused talents and gifts. According to the Bible, *"a lazy man does not roast his prey, but the precious possession of a man is diligence. In the way of righteousness is life, and in its pathway there is no death"* *[Proverbs 12:27-28, Proverbs 10:4 and 12:24].*

The lazy man may not want to get out of their bed *[Proverbs 13:4, 15:19].* Laziness may contribute to unnecessary increase in weight problems which might trigger other medical conditions.

There are many types of laziness including work related laziness, spiritual laziness, financial laziness and physical laziness all of which ends up opening loop holes for the enemies in the life of the lazy person. The cure for every type of laziness is hard work. First, we need to identify which type of laziness we suffer from, seek for the truth on this identified laziness and then set out to work to overcome it with God on our side. For we 'can do all things through Christ who strengthens us'. *[Philippians 4:13].*

The Bible admonishes the sluggard in Proverbs 6 to go to the ants and learn its ways. For a start, ants are so small in size and unnoticeable as they go about their daily chores. A close look at the ant will confirm that success in life does not depend on physical strength or age but it depends on wisdom, the source of which is God. The ants prepare their food and shelter a long time before the rainy or winter season arrives. They work tirelessly to prepare for adverse weather conditions by extended food gathering and storing in their various chambers. As tiny as the ants may be, they have techniques for moving food or any objects that are much bigger than their size and weight even when it means getting others to join in the move. The worker ant hardly gives up on its mission. If and when there are big obstacles on its way, it climbs one side and descends on the other or goes round it, remaining focused on its mission.

No obstacle should deter us from accomplishing our God-given assignment. Once an ant finds a source of food, it is able to accurately return to same source time after time without losing its bearing. An ant knows how to pass information on where the food or drink is to other ants. It willingly shares useful information and extends its nets far and wide in search of food and water. With the ants, there is a lot of recycling so little if anything is wasted. The ants work in harmony to build a lasting ant hill. Ants are very hard working and are teachable.

How many able bodied people in some communities would rather depend on the state to feed and clothe them instead of going to work or create work for themselves and others? How many of us are meek and humble and have teachable spirits? Life is full of challenges and obstacles. How many of us are willing to pay the price for success in our God assigned task?

Thoughts

Every good or positive invention and bad or negative invention started from someone's thought. The power of the effect of our thought on us cannot be quantified. Whoever or whatever captures anyone's thought captures that person's life. No wonder the Bible says we must guard our thoughts for from it flow the rivers of life. Have you noticed that actions or inactions mostly follow our thoughts? Sometimes we react or act based on the information that we have and been processing in our thoughts previously. If the enemy can attack your thought and rule your mind then you are defeated. To overcome ungodly thoughts, we must prayerfully focus on the word of God, anchoring our thoughts on the infallible word of God either spoken or written in the Bible. We need to fellowship more with the Holy Spirit moment by moment, being mindful and careful about what we hear in words and music and careful about what we say to each other and to ourselves. As a man thinketh in his heart so he is *[Proverbs 23:7]*.

I'll like to share this with you, *"Finally, brothers and sisters, whatever is true, whatever is noble, whatever is right, whatever is pure, whatever is lovely, whatever is admirable – if anything is excellent or praiseworthy think about such things. Whatever you have learned or received or heard from me, or seen in me put it into practice. And the God of peace will be with you"* [Philippians 4:8-9]

Unbelief

Believe in the Lord your God so shall ye be established; believe His prophets so shall ye prosper. 2Chronicles 20:20b. Unbelief is the opposite of believe or faith in someone or something. It is the eraser that wipes out any prayer request and faith in its potency. Unbelief is one of the reasons for not seeing or receiving miracles even today. Jesus could not do much in his hometown for the people did not believe in Him. *Matthew 13:53-58, Mark 6:1-6.* We need to put our faith and belief in God for who He is, for what He says and does. *Mark 9:14-27.* Peter by faith in Jesus Christ walked on the water but other disciples did not have enough faith or courage to ask or venture out.

We need to believe in God-led and God-sent prophets. *1John 4:1, 1Thessalonians 5:21. 1 Samuel 9–10:11. 2 Chronicles 20:1-29.* Unbelief in God and his prophets could be disastrous. *2 Kings 7:1-20.*

We need to believe in ourselves that God at our creation has input in us all that we need to succeed in life. Equally in the name, strength and power of the Lord, we can be strong and do exploits that perhaps no one in our families have ever done before, *Judges 6-7:8.* We can do all things through Christ who strengthens us. *Philippians 4:13.* It is bad for others not to trust us but it is most painful when we do not believe in ourselves. We need to shake off all unbelief in God, His prophet and in ourselves.

Love

We cannot afford to be our own arch enemy. The one that fights against his team mates cannot win. We need to love ourselves the best we can whilst trusting God to make us perfect in every way. You and I should be our best friend, our number one fan, cheer leader and well wisher. We must learn to consciously and unconditionally love ourselves. We may not love some things that we do but we ought to love ourselves as we work together with the Holy Spirit on daily basis. Don't we often put ourselves down in how we look, what we do or our achievements through His Grace, often preferring others and loving others in so many ways more than ourselves? Sometimes it is not what other people say to us that get us down but what we say to ourselves.

How often do we praise ourselves in modesty or give ourselves a treat at the end of the day, week, and school time or after an achievement? Don't we find it difficult or impossible to encourage ourselves in the Lord like David did especially in hard times? [1 Samuel 30:6]. We owe it to God to love others just like we love ourselves. We must stop focusing on our weak points –that is not to say to neglect them but to say we need to spend more time and resources to focus on our strengths. Permit me to share with you a write-up that I read a while ago from the Word for Today 2000 © Bob Gass.

12 Healthy Attitudes Towards Myself

- I know God created me and that He loves me – *Jeremiah 31:3*

- I have shortcomings and I want to change. I believe that God is working in my life each day; while He is, I can still accept and enjoy myself.
- Everyone has faults, I am not a failure because I am not perfect.
- I am working with God to overcome my faults, but there will always be something to work on; therefore I will not be discouraged when He convicts me of an area that need improvement.
- I want people to like me but my sense of worth is not dependent on them. Jesus has already demonstrated my worth by dying for me.
- I will not be controlled by what others say, think or do. If they reject me I will survive, for God has promised never to reject me as long as I keep on believing.
- No matter how often I fail I will not give up, because God is with me, He has promised to strengthen and to sustain me as long as I live *[Hebrews 13:5]*.
- I like myself, I do not like everything I do, and I want to change - but I refuse to put myself down.
- I am acceptable to God through the blood of Jesus *[Ephesians 2:8-9]*.
- God has a plan for my life and I am going to fulfill it; I have God given gifts and I intend to use them to glorify Him.
- I myself, I am nothing, but in Christ I am everything I need to be.
- I can do whatever God calls me to do, through the powers of Him who dwells in me *[Philippians 4:14]* Amen.

Self Abuse

This is self inflicted injury that manifests in many ways ranging from inflicting injuries upon oneself using sharp instruments such as razor blades, deliberate cigarette or iron burns, to overdosing oneself with drugs such as pain killers e.g. paracetamol. Such a person often suffers from low self esteem or rejection etc. They may want to die thinking life is not worth living but this is all the lie of the devil.

Some because of the fear of poverty, secondary to loneliness, avoiding relationships, stressful relationships at home, avoiding responsibilities at home, low self esteem, infertility – coming to an empty home, proving or wanting to prove to themselves and others etc. have become work-alcoholics forgetting that too much work without any play makes Jack a dull boy. God desires for us to rest too. He rested on the seventh day.

Some either by trying to be acceptable by their peers or friends or colleagues or because of socializing have become alcoholics while others think they can drink their sorrows away. They forget that once they become sober, the reality of their problem will come back plus perhaps medical and financial problems of significant consequences.

Whatever self abuse you may be experiencing, it needs to be recognized as such, the reasons for it identified and addressed. Love yourself enough to seek for godly counselling and mentoring. Be willing and prepared to commit to changes, be open and honest in your communications with your mentor and counsellor so that the help you will receive will be the most appropriate for your situation.

May we pray please?

Prayer Points:
- Lord, please deliver me from every single wrong association or advice that has or is leading me away from You.
- Father, only in Your Mercy, deliver me from every sinful habit and attitude including uncontrolled anger, backbiting, gossip, stealing, self abuse etc. that might want to mar my character and bring shame to Your Holy name.
- Lord, please purify my thoughts from now so that it will be in line with Your word and purpose for my life,
- Deliver me, Father, from every seed and root of procrastination. Do please help me to stand up from my slumber and do all that I need to do on time to Your own Glory and Honour.
- Father, help me never again take You for granted on any issue however small or trivial. Help me Lord to be more appreciative of Your daily load of blessings. Help me also to be thankful to my family, friends and destiny helpers.
- Father, how I need Your help 24/7 on how to avoid

SELF

laziness in all my ways and undertakings as from now in Jesus' name I pray and with thanksgiving. Amen.

For us to overcome the enemy of self, we need to ask the Lord to come into our lives i.e. to be 'born again". We need to realize that life is war. It is not unusual for our flesh to want things or do things that may not be entirely helpful to us. It is not unusual to find ourselves doing the same things that we dislike or hate and vice versa. It happened to great people before including Paul *[Romans 7]*. We need to cooperate with the Holy Spirit to develop our spirit man and learn to daily subject our flesh to be controlled by the Spirit of God in us [*Romans 7:15-25, 8:1-14]*.

Before you and I again pray the 'fall down and die'[3] prayer for our enemies, we ought to take a look and make sure that we ourselves are not the enemies we are praying against.

Dear friend, who truly is your enemy and how will you overcome this enemy?

---

[3] This is a prayer pattern currently making waves amongst Christians, especially in Nigeria, where the person praying commands his/her perceived enemies and/or demons to *fall down and die!* The fall down and die prayer is a fruitless one in light of the enemy called "self" because often times, when we pray that prayer, we are actually chasing shadows and refusing to take responsibility for our own acts of omission or commission. Rather than point the finger at our imaginary enemies and/or demons, we ought to pay attention to the little foxes within us that spoil our vine by ensuring that we master the inadequacies in our thoughts, character and actions. The irony of this prayer is that demons are spirit beings and they do not die but the Bible encourages us to *die to self!* Death to the enemy called self, is the only way to conquering this dangerous but often overlooked enemy of humanity.

CHAPTER 11
SELECTED POEMS

1. AS A MAN THINKS — 87
2. IT'S MY LIFE — 90
3. FEAR — 91
4. HE FORGAVE ME — 93
5. I WILL LIFT UP MY EYES (PSALMS 121) — 95
6. SIN — 98
7. THE DEAD END — 101
8. 'THY WILL BE DONE ON LORD' — 103
9. DO YOU LOVE YOURSELF? — 106

SELECTED POEMS

AS A MAN THINKS

As a man thinks so he is, goes the saying
What is the size of your God?
What is the limit of the Glory of your God?
What are the limitations of His power, presence and personality?
Who is He to you each time?

When you think about the Almighty God
What sort of thoughts do you have about Him?
What sort of image do you have in your mind?
What sort of limitations do you attribute to Him?
What sort of inspiration do you receive from Him?

As a man thinks of His God so he receives
Your ability to receive great and mighty gifts
Your ability to continually be in His presence
Your privilege to remain in fellowship
All depends on who your God is.

If you think your God is very small
Then you should be contented with small things
If you think your God is very, very big
Then you will agree that nothing is bigger than Him.
No matter what the problem or circumstance might be.

THE ENEMY WITHIN

Many of us have ignorantly complained about God
When we have been the main cause of our problems
We accuse Him of things He will not do
We leave Him out of minor and major decisions
We limit our God's power, purpose and prerogatives.

Friend, your thinking has affected you thus far
Such that you are full of many negative thoughts
No wonder you don't get anything done and on time
Such that your confessions are depressing and sad
No wonder you have lived a miserable, unproductive life.

Why will you continue to think negatively and small?
Why will you refuse God's gift of possible intervention?
Why will you remain carnal in your thinking?
Why refuse to broaden your imagination of God?
Why continue to focus your thinking on your circumstances?

As a man thinks so he really is.
If you will humbly ask God to help you brother
To create in you a new clean heart today
Filled with clean thoughts and right desires
Then will your mountain of problems be levelled.

SELECTED POEMS

As a man thinks so he is.
You no longer have any sincere excuse
Not to possess your possession right away
Will you today reconsider your moment-by-moment thoughts
For indeed as a man thinks so he really is.

© *O. Ola – Ojo Proverbs 23:7 Dec.' 90*

IT'S MY LIFE

'It's my life' you say and you are correct
'I can live just the way I want and choose'
Sleeping all day instead of going to school or work
Watching the television twenty-four seven
Staying on the 'dole' instead of seeking for employment
Partying, clubbing instead of studying or working
Sleeping around with whomever and whenever
Instead of keeping your body a temple for God
Overeating instead of eating moderately
Overworking instead of taking adequate rest
It's my life you keep saying to yourself and others.

'It's my life' you say and you are correct
Friend, remember it is indeed your life
Once you choose your behaviour
You have chosen the reward of your behaviour
Time now to reconsider, time now to re-think
For you have just one life
Why end up in pain and shame?
Why live in abject poverty and starve,
When God has a better place and plan for you?
It's your life so make the best of it friend.

© O.Ola-Ojo 14.06.08

FEAR

Many of us exercise fear once in a while
For some others, they fear virtually everything
But the question keeps coming to my mind
What is fear, why and what do people fear?

Fear is s feeling of unpleasant consequences
Should something negative happen at any given time.
Fear is real to the individual being involved
But then should one continue to live on constant fear?

Many fear sickness of any kind or type
Maybe because of the previous experience of theirs
Some fear the thought of dying at a young age
For they are not certain about their eternity.

Many fear being involved in any accident
Be it domestic or road traffic accident
This is because many a times such an accident
Leaves the victim with permanent injuries.

Many fear being left in total darkness
Whilst some fear being left alone anywhere
Others fear being involved with a crowd
For some their fear is heights or rivers.

THE ENEMY WITHIN

Why are you constantly fearful dearly beloved?
What are those circumstances that put fear into you?
Fear could be dangerous to your well being in all ways
What then is the solution to this instrument of the devil?

Many people fear because of their ignorance
Ignorance about their circumstances or (and) problems
Ignorance about God and His ample provisions
They for a long time are under Satan's grip.

The fear of the Lord the scripture says
Is the beginning of wisdom to mankind
Fear of any man is a dangerous trap
To trust the Lord means safety.

The wicked run whilst nobody is pursuing them
But the godly are as bold and fearless as lions
For God has not given to any the spirit of fear
But of love, sound mind and power to His own.

© O. Ola - Ojo 19/8/89.
[2 Timothy 1:7, Proverbs 1: 7-9, 29:25, Isaiah 8:13].

HE FORGAVE ME

I should have been at the battlefield
Fighting for my King and His people
At home I got very bored
Decided to talk a walk on my balcony.

I saw the beautiful woman in the shower
Couldn't take my eyes and mind off her
I must have her I kept thinking
Instructed my servants to get her for me.

I could not resist her beauty in her clothes
Passionately and secretly I made love to her
That she was another man's wife didn't matter
Sent her home with some usual gifts I thought.

Weeks later my sins caught up with me
My secret lover was carrying my seed I learnt
A seed that couldn't be stopped from growing
Soon it will be seen and the truth will be out.

I must find a way to cover up my mistake
All attempts to deceive her husband failed
He was a much God fearing man than I
I had to organise his death with my army general.

THE ENEMY WITHIN

He died as I had planned and hoped what a relief!
I had it all sorted out I breathed a sigh of relief
Into my palace I brought my once secret lover
Now to become my legitimate wife and lover.

He saw it all I had forgotten and He sent me a word
The prophet came with His judgement too hard to bear
My son became suddenly very ill, I cried to Him
Too late for he died because of my wicked acts.

I confessed my sins to Him for my lust and wickedness
I repented of all the evil I had done to date known to me
I made up my mind never to repeat that sin again
He heard my confessions, cries and petitions at last.

He forgave me, He forgave me and He forgave me
However at a costly price to myself, family now and later
My secret sins were to be openly punished and rewarded
He forgave me, He forgave me and He forgave me.

Friend however bad or horrible your sins might be
Whoever you have killed or maimed before now
If you will acknowledge and confess your sins to Him
He who forgave me will forgive you too.

© O.Ola – Ojo. Samuel 11 – 12:19.

I WILL LIFT UP MY EYES
(PSALMS 121)

I will lift up my eyes to the mountains;
from whence shall my help come?

Lord when I look at the mountains,
They seem way high up above; solid, strong and
immovable.
My help however cannot come from the mountains
As they are without life themselves.

My help comes from the Lord, who
made heaven and earth.

Lord in times past, my help has come from You,
Maker of heaven and earth.
Even though You are my Father and Lord by
creative and redemptive rights,
Yet it seems You are so far away from me at the moment
As my cries to You for help has not been answered.
If You would help me,
I know none of Your creatures can stand in
my way of progress.
Right now, I need Your help against my adversaries and
oppressors
who to me appear way high up like the mountains.

THE ENEMY WITHIN

***He will not allow my foot to slip, He who
keeps me will not slumber.
Behold He who keeps Israel will neither
slumber nor sleep.***

Lord, these words express how vulnerable I am without
Your help.
These days I cannot feel You holding my hands and
I fear that my foot is about to slip.
Much as I believe that You do not sleep nor slumber,
To lose Your grip on me,
Yet I do not feel Your hold as before and as a child I am
frightened,
And feel completely alone and abandoned.

***The Lord is my keeper. The Lord is my
shade on my right.
The Sun will not smite me by day nor
the moon by night.***

Thank You Lord for being my keeper.
You have been my protector in times past.
Please come and once again be a shade for me
From the surrounding heat of oppression, injustice,
wickedness,
poverty, failure, loss and loneliness
So that I might not be smitten by them in Jesus' name.

SELECTED POEMS

The Lord will protect me from all evil.
He will keep my soul.

Please Lord protect me according to Your promise
from all forms of evil
Including unbelief and pride,
Which may want to attack my soul at this time of great need
And keep my soul from denying You.

The Lord will guard my going in and coming out
from this time forth and ever more.

Thank You Lord for the promise of guarding my ways
And being with me forever.
As I daily go about my duties and tasks,
May I experience Your leading and protection once more
and always
In Jesus name (Amen).

© O. Ola - Ojo. 1995.

SIN

What is your definition of sin, dear friend?
In a changing society like ours with changing ideologies,
Many have removed the word 'sin' form their dictionary,
To them it is one of those acceptable societal norms.

Sin to me, is not an illness, dear friend,
It is neither a temptation nor problem,
It is not a mistake or normal,
It is that which is done of our choice.

Sin has a love and hatred relationship,
Men tend to love its false pleasures,
Hating themselves, or others, thereafter,
It is that which requires forgiveness.

Sin is dabbled into deliberately and consciously
It becomes addictive over time like a drug,
It never satisfies, no matter how much the amount,
It tends to be covered up with other sins.

Sin is incredibly destructive, dear friend;
It is the most expensive thing in this world,
It causes sickness and death of all kinds,
It finally sends the unrepentant sinner to Hell's fire.

SELECTED POEMS

Sin causes a person untold loss of relationship,
It causes breaks in human relationships;
It causes communication breakdown with God;
It causes one to lose one's dignity, peace and respect.

Sin, expensive, as it was, had to be purchased,
It cost God His only begotten Son Jesus Christ;
It caused Jesus to leave Heaven and come to earth;
It caused Jesus to lay down His life on the cross.

Sin is sin in the sight of God, no matter what your excuse
It is an abomination in the sight of God,
It will be punished sooner or later, dear friend,
It is full of deadly poison and toxins.

Sin requires forgiveness first from God,
It does require admitting it and confessing it,
It requires our complete round about turn to good;
It requires a conscious effort to forsake it through the Holy Spirit.

Sin's forgiveness first is from the Almighty God,
It needs forgiveness from those affected by it,
It needs the sinner forgiving himself or herself;
It needs the blood of Jesus for complete cleansing.

Societal acceptance of that sin as a common norm,
Does not remove it from being sin in God's presence,
It does not remove its gravity or punishment,
Indeed the soul that sinneth will surely die.

THE ENEMY WITHIN

Will you, dear friend, continue to toy with that sin?
Will you not remember that God is seeing it?
Will you stop refusing to admit this abomination?
Will you not today do away with that sin completely?

© O. Ola-Ojo 1992.

THE DEAD END

It starts like any other useful, straight forward road
It looks so beautiful and very attractive
Very promising is the quality at the beginning
With promising signs to a destination at last.

What an unfortunate mistake to travel on it
What seemed initially attractive and beautiful
What seemed unending and everlasting
Turns out to be just one of the dead ends.

Every sin dear friend is a dead end
For in the end it is full of disgrace and regrets
Full of heartaches, uncertainty and hatred
Full of bitterness, pity and unaccountable loss.

No matter how small or big that sin is
No matter where, when and how it was committed
No matter whatever excuse we might want to give
It does not remove the sin from being the dead end.

The dead end has nothing to really offer you friend
It has no guarantee, no security nor peace
It has no degree of commitment or improvement
It has no hope for a better future friend.

THE ENEMY WITHIN

Now is the time to retrace back your steps friend
Now is the time to reassess the situation again
Now is the time to seek the Lord's face once more
In order that you might not end up in the dead end.

In your daily walk in life dearly beloved
Do try and watch out for the dead end
Do not be attracted to it or trapped in it
For ultimately it is going to be the dead end.

© O.Ola –Ojo 11.03.92.

SELECTED POEMS

'THY WILL BE DONE OH LORD'

When like precious Joseph I am being abandoned
By those who are supposed to be very close to me Lord
Help me to keep doing all the good I know unto others
Looking forward to a breakthrough someday saying,
'Thy will be done oh Lord'.

When at the war front against 'Goliath' I am prepared
like David
And I am being offered all physical, man made weapons
Lord
Help me to remember that the arms of flesh will
certainly fail
With boldness only in Your Words may I say,
'Thy will be done oh Lord'.

When all hope has been lost like that of Jonah the
Prophet
And in the submarine of discomfort, problems and
uncertainty I find myself
Remind me of Your promise that You will make all things
work for good
And right there may I confidently say,
'Thy will be done oh Lord'.

When I am seriously tempted to give up in my faith
In Your previous, precious revelations to me dear Lord

THE ENEMY WITHIN

Remind me only of my past experiences and Your faithfulness
With a heart full of gratitude may I say,
'Thy will be done oh Lord'.

When I am fed up with my job and my environment
And I feel rightly justified to do so dear Lord
Help me to remember how many souls You have blessed
In the process of my stay saying,
'Thy will be done oh Lord'.

When my friends and family cannot understand me
And I cannot explain what I am doing and why Lord
Help me to remember that You are still leading me
Unto Your expected end and say,
'Thy will be done oh Lord'.

When I am at the cross- road, unsure of what to do
And the vision seems to be tarrying on what next Lord
Help me to remember Your ever present presence with me
Communing with You and saying,
'Thy will be done oh Lord'.

When I have to suffer for the sake of the precious gospel
And in the eyes of people I become a laughing stock
Remind me of Jesus Christ's experience of the cross
Boldly bearing the suffering saying,
'Thy will be done oh Lord'.

SELECTED POEMS

When You are asking me Lord to do certain things
Things that are contrary to my own taste and nature
Remind me that Your ways are not my ways Lord.
Obediently and willingly may I say,
'Thy will be done oh Lord'.

When I have to give up things that are precious to me
Starting all over again in a new unknown environment
Missing all my good old friends, colleagues and loving neighbours
Thankful unto Thee may I say
'Thy will be done oh Lord'.

© O.Ola-Ojo '90
Luke 22 : 42.

DO YOU LOVE YOURSELF?

Love your neighbour as yourself
Is the Biblical injunction to all
But the question comes to mind
Do you love yourself dear friend?

Many want to love their neighbours
As themselves many a times
Yet they do not love themselves
Enough to transfer this love to others.

You have been hearing the salvation message
Over and over again from many people
Do you love yourself enough to accept
Jesus Christ as your Lord and Saviour?

Do you love yourself as a child in the home
Respecting your parents and those older than you?
Do you fulfil all your family obligations
To merit a long life full of blessing?.

Do you love yourself as a student
In your attendance at lectures?
Is your submission of assignments timely?
How hard do you study for examinations?

Do you love yourself in your marital relationship?
Is your marriage based on God's principles?
Is it based on monogamy and permanency?
Is it based on fidelity and love?

God has blessed you with riches and talents
Do you love yourself enough to give them back to Him
As you give willingly to the spread of the gospel?
And wisely utilise your talents to bless mankind?

Do you love yourself in your self evaluations?
Are your confessions negative or positive?
Is your thought true, pure, lovely, good and right?
How much do you pray for yourself?

Self is one's greatest enemy
The flesh lusts against the spirit
What you want to do that you don't do
What you don't want is what you do.

'Charity begins at home' is the saying of the wise
Start to love yourself from now
In your thoughts, utterances and actions
Then loving your neighbour will be easy for you.

© O.Ola-Ojo
Philippians 4:8, Matthew 19:19 & Romans 8:21-25.

Dear Reader,

Thank you for your time and resources committed to supporting this writing ministry. Please help to tell others about how much the Lord has blessed you reading this book.

You will certainly be blessed by the other books written by Oluwakemi, so why not visit www.protokospublishers.co.uk and place an order today.

It will equally be appreciated if you can help to write a few sentences review of the book on www.amazon.com and/or on www.protokospublishers.co.uk

Please note that all our books are easily available on our website and other good bookshops.

God bless you as you do.
Management
Protokos Publishers.

OPPORTUNITY TO BECOME A CHRISTIAN

Dear Father in heaven,
Thank you for the privilege of reading this book. Indeed I have sinned and come short of Your glory. I am grateful to You for sending Jesus Christ into this world to come to die on the cross of Calvary for me. I believe in my heart that Jesus Christ paid for my sins, past, present and future. I believe Jesus Christ was buried and on the third day He rose from the dead. I believe that Jesus Christ will come back again. I confess with my mouth and I accept Him now to be my Lord.

Master, Saviour, Brother, and Friend, I ask in Your mercy for the infilling of the Holy Spirit so that with His help, I can live a victorious life becoming all that You have ordained me to be in Jesus' name. I pray with thanksgiving. Amen.

CONGRATULATIONS YOU ARE BORN AGAIN!

If after reading this book you said the above prayer and became born-again, Congratulations! You are Born Again is a booklet for those who have done so through reading this book. It is a free booklet that we would like you to have. In it, the frequently asked questions are answered and this will get you on the way to growing in your newfound faith in God. You can download this free booklet from our website: **www.protokospublishers.co.uk**

You may also contact any of the organisations listed at the end of the book.

I look forward to hearing from you soon.
O. Ola-Ojo (2012)

OTHER BOOKS.

Other Books By The Author:

Provocation, Prayer and Praise
(December 2004 & 2009)

Complimentary to The Christian and Infertility this book focuses on the story of an infertile woman in the Bible, her provocations, prayer and praise. Whatever makes you incomplete, unfulfilled, less than whom God made you to be, whatever issue of life that the enemy uses to provoke you calls for prayer.

Key features include:
- Some known medical reasons for infertility in the women.
- Why Hannah went to the house of God in spite of her barrenness.
- Is it true that the husband is much more than 10 sons to the infertile woman?
- When, where and how to address the source/cause of your provocation.
- God is able to meet that humanly impossible need of yours.
- God's part and your part in that promise.
- Time to celebrate and praise God.

Book Details:
Paperback: 128 pages
Language English
ISBN-13: 978-0-9557898-3-0

Review:
An excellent easy to read and understand book. The principles shared in this book though primarily are for those trying for a baby could as well be applied to any area of hurt and un-fulfillment.

Reviewer: A Reader from London, 7 Jan 2006 on Amazon.co.uk

 :www.protokospublishers.co.uk

OTHER BOOKS.

The Christian and Infertility
(December 2004 & 2009)

The Christian and Infertility addresses one of the often neglected needs of Christian couples. It gives an insight into infertility from the biblical and medical perspectives. It is written not only for potential fruitful couples but for pastors, family and friends of these couples. It is written that the Body of Christ might be fully equipped to know and support couples who are facing the challenge of infertility at present

Key features include:
- Childlessness in the Bible and lessons to learn;
- Some known spiritual causes of infertility;
- The man and low sperm count;
- Some possible physical, medical and environmental causes of infertility;
- Some of the available treatment options in the UK;
- Choice of fertility treatment;
- Should a Christian professional be involved in fertility treatment?

Book Details:
Paperback: 146 pages
Language English
ISBN-13: 978-0-9557898-2-3

Review:
The book is a great eye-opener for all. It sheds light on infertility from the medical and spiritual angle. This gives the reader a balance because i believe every human being is made up of both physical and spiritual part. To get a balance in life, the two parts must be well fed. One must not concentrate on the spiritual and neglect the physical part. The book also reminds us that God has a way of sorting us out. The book is quite inspiring. I will recommend this book to everybody trusting God for any form of blessing from God to go get one and apply it to his or her situation. It will definitely bless you and yours'.

Reviewer: A reader from Glen Burnie, USA, 29 Oct 2007 on Amazon.co.uk

 :www.protokospublishers.co.uk

OTHER BOOKS.

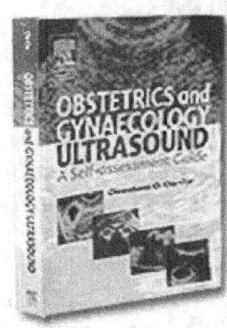

Obstetrics and Gynaecology Ultrasound -
A Self-Assessment Guide
June 2005 Churchill Elsevier Publishers, UK.

This self-assessment guide is a structured questions and answer book that develops the reader's understanding capability using a simple method in treating related topics. Clinical indications are presented with their corresponding ultrasound findings using appropriate illustrations. A case study approach is followed; presenting the clinical and ethical dilemmas that might arise whilst encouraging students to think.
The aim is to reinforce theoretical knowledge within a clinical environment.

Key features:
- Includes a detailed study of fertility.
- Aids quick understanding of subject matter.
- Over 600 high-resolution ultrasound images.
- Cover a wide spectrum of ultrasound curriculum.

Book Details:
- Paperback: 468 pages
- ISBN-10: 0443064628
- ISBN-13: 978-0443064623

Review:
"...This excellent new book is a study guide... This is an attractive paperback that should be essential reading for trainee obstetric and gynaecological sonographers, whether they are radiographers or radiology or obstetric trainees. It will be of particular value to those preparing for the RCOG/RCR Diploma in Advanced Obstetric Ultrasound and to specialist registrars in obstetrics and gynaecology undertaking special skills modules in fetal medicine, gynaecological ultrasound and infertility..."

The Obstetrician & Gynaecologist, www.rcog.org.uk/togonline
Book reviews 2006

Reviewer : Ann Harper MD FRCPI FRCOG.
Consultant Obstetrician and Gynaecologist
Royal Jubilee Maternity Service, Belfast., UK

 :www.protokospublishers.co.uk

OTHER BOOKS.

GOOD MUMS, BAD MUMS
(June 2005 & 2009)

This is in two parts, the main chapter that can be used for personal or group study, and an accompanying exercise section. The privileged position of a mother is in her being a co-creator with God and bringing forth life (lives). This book compliments one of God's previous revelations to me as contained in the book titled Good Dads, Bad Dads'. While the father could be likened to the pilot of the family plane, the mother can be likened to the force behind the plane – positive or negative. Good mothers are not only co-creators with God, they also do nurture as well as nourish their children physically, emotionally and spiritually.

Keys Features:
- Were all the mothers in the Bible good mothers?
- Be motivated in the areas of your strengths.
- Learn ways of supporting your husband and children.
- Lessons from the strengths and weakness of 7 mothers.
- Be encouraged - you are not alone in the assignment of motherhood.

Book Details:
- Paperback: 162 pages
- Language : English
- ISBN-13: 978-0-9557898-1-6

Review:
I appreciate the author's method of writing. It is always exciting holding her book to read. Personally, 'Good Mums, Bad Mums' has been a blessing to me in no small measure. The book is rich, it is loaded with physical and spiritual uplifting subjects. To all existing and potential mothers, this book is a MUST read. At the end of every chapter there is an exercise to do that will help in re-examining your life spiritually and in other ways. I encourage all women to get and use this book as a guide in raising their children. You will be glad you did.

Reviewer: Pastor Mrs T Adegoke
Freedom Arena
London, UK

 :www.protokospublishers.co.uk

OTHER BOOKS.

To the Bride with Love
(2007 & 2009)

Every wise woman preparing to get married knows she will need sound advice, practical tips and solid, heartfelt prayers, of those who have travelled on the road she is about to journey on. In this book, 10 women of different age groups, from different backgrounds and cultures who wedded under various circumstances, individually share their experience with the bride in an intimate, very candid and unforgettable way

Keys Features:
- Learn from 10 married women.
- Find your divine purpose in marriage.
- Learn what and how to feed your family.
- Be blessed by prayers from your guests.
- Receive remarkable gifts for your marriage.

Book details:
Paperback: 108 pages
Language: English
ISBN-13: 978-0-9557898-4-7

To the Bride with Love is the perfect bride's evergreen companion. The content is suitable, relevant and applicable even decades after the wedding day.

To the Bride with Love is an ideal wedding gift on its own. It can also accompany any other gift (big or small) that you have for the bride but take this hint... the bride will keep thanking you for the book years and years after.

Reviews:
'One of the best', This book has really helped my marriage from the onset as I got it as a wedding gift, God bless the giver. It's a must read for relationship improvement and God's guidance. I recommend it for people to get it for themselves, moreover as a great blessing for someone else in love. "To the Bride with Love"
Reviewer: **Sade Olaoye** "clare4good" (United Kingdom) 19 Jul 2008 on Amazon.com

OTHER BOOKS.

Another Review:

The writing style of Oluwakemi is unique, peculiar and distinct to herself. I recommend To the Bride with Love to wives, wives to be, mothers, mentors, youth leaders and workers. Why? The clarity, the focus and the intent of this book is so empowering, encouraging and enlightening that it will definitely mold or re mold a life to achieve its purpose. The truth is, there are very few books that have depth as well as help you to achieve your goals and arrive at your destination. Many books tend to excite you but have no depth; you read and you forget; they do not really change you but this book, To the Bride with Love will definitely leave a word in your spirit and move you to your next level!

I believe that this is also a book that pastors will find useful as a manual for marriage counseling, because many books on marriage focus mostly on what you as an individual can gain, your own personal satisfaction while little is said about the sacrifices involved and their importance. As my pastor usually says, it is important to learn from those who have gone ahead, understand why some were successful and others weren't, so that we won't fall where they fell, rather, we would gain more speed, achieve our goals and thereby glorify Christ.

So, I invite you not only to get a copy of this life-changing manual for yourself, but also to put it into as many hands as you can afford to, for then the world will definitely benefit and your life will be a blessing to many.

Reviewer: Oyinlola Odunlami CEO.
Shallom Bookshop, London UK

:www.protokospublishers.co.uk

OTHER BOOKS.

Refuge Under His Wings

"an exhaustive analysis of the Book of Ruth in the Bible. The author combines her deep Christian conviction and excellent knowledge of the Holy Scriptures to produce a must read for every Christian, married or single. The book is interspaced with beautifully written prayers, which enables the reader to pause, pray and meditate on the revelations received... The book is also loaded with poetry like 'Thy will be done oh Lord' for those who may be facing an uncertain future or on a cross road of decisions."

Key Features:
- Famine in the land whose fault?
- Do I relocate in famine times and where to?
- Back to God, back to blessings.
- Finding refuge Under His Wings.
- A new beginning and a new song

Book details:
Paperback: 100 pages
Language: English
ISBN-10: 095578980X
ISBN-13: 978-0955789809

Review:
This book feeds the soul. Most of all I loved the poetry. It gives you time to savour the thoughts as reader. There is a good mix of poetry and prose. To look at the story of Ruth in depth gave good spiritual food. You can pause and take it in at your own pace. The meditation on Psalm 121 was good also. There's nothing like reading a Psalm slowly and meditating on its contents. The author's own reflections allow you to see the book through someone else's eyes. A good read.

Reviewer : Gaby Richards,
London, UK.

 :www.protokospublishers.co.uk

Other Books.

GRACE OR WORKS?

OLUWAKEMI O. OLA-OJO

This book makes you examine a lot of issues in your life, family relationships in particular, that you may have taken for granted or totally ignored. As conveyed right from the rhetorical question posed in the title, Grace or Works, the author stirs you towards asking yourself pertinent questions, thinking through for answers and even getting solutions for unresolved problems.

Have you heard of prodigal wives, husbands, mothers or prodigal fathers? This book identifies and defines them clearly. For anyone experiencing a crises in their relationship with such prodigal family members, this book, which is based on the parable of the "Prodigal son" in Luke 15:11-32 is a one-stop resource material to meet your counseling needs. And just in case you happen to be the prodigal who has caused your relatives much sorrow, there is hope for you in this book.

Interspersed with prayers for you by the author and specific prayers that you can say for yourself, as well as poems to comfort and inspire you, Grace or Works not only asks you questions, it helps you make and maintain the right choices.

Key Features:
- Right request but wrong timing.
- God's gifting and our free will.
- Abroad but for the wrong reasons.
- Time to return home.
- A father's unmerited favour.
- 'Shut out' of celebrations because of anger.
- You did not have because you did not ask.

Book details:
Paperback: 122 pages
Language: English
ISBN-13: 978-0-9557898-5-4

 :www.protokospublishers.co.uk

OTHER BOOKS.

THERE IS A REWARD FOR PARENTING

Man may claim that the conception of a particular child was accidental, but in God's eyes every child is in His plan and has a purpose and mission to fulfill here on earth. As a parent, teacher, church or community leader, how are you treating the children in your care?

God does not sleep nor slumber; are you sure you are doing what He expects of you as a parent or children's Sunday school teacher? What kind of reward do you expect from Him?

There is a Reward for Parenting provides a lot of answers and food for thought, using scriptural principles to show you how to ensure a good reward from God in the unique assignment of parenting and child care.

As characteristic of Oluwakemi Ola-Ojo's previous books, there is a free gift of her poems at the end of this book also, to add value to the content of the main text – making it two books for the price of one!

Key Features:
- Every child counts.
- The making of a winner.
- You need wisdom.
- Good and bad parenting.

Book details:
Paperback: 88 pages
Language : English
ISBN 978-0-9557898-6-1

Review:
The book is lovely, inspiring, very educative both spiritually and secularly.

Reviewer : **M.F.Owoeye**. Lagos- Nigeria

 :www.protokospublishers.co.uk

OTHER BOOKS.

Let's Reason Together ...Youths' A-Z (Book 1)

According to the United Nations demographic statistics, the global youth population, ranging in age from 15 to 24 years, today stands at more than 1.5 billion, representing about 22 percent or a fifth of the world's 6.8 billion people inhabiting the earth. In developing nations where a greater number of this group resides, the youth population sometimes gets as high as 60% or more of the total population of such nations!

Since it is also globally accepted that the youth of any nation forms the strength of that nation, economically, militarily and/or otherwise, it is imperative that this group of people cannot be overlooked.

It is against this backdrop that the book, **LET'S REASON TOGETHER – YOUTH'S A-Z** is a timely one that is set to address the various issues that affect young people as well as their vision and aspirations. Since the primary goal of young people is to live full lives in their societies, this book examines specific elements that would help them in this process. It covers a wide range of issues from the sublime such as attitude, choices, education, health and xenophobia to the seemingly mundane such as dreams, integrity and vacation.

Key Features:
- A relevant word per alphabet.
- A time to reflect on the key word.
- An easy phrase per alphabet to remember.
- 3 prayer points per alphabet to help you pray.

Book details:
- Paperback: 316 pages
- ISBN 978-0-9557898-7-8

Review:
This is the most wonderful piece of youth work I have ever seen, capturing diverse situations and circumstances peculiar to youths. The work is thorough, educative and spiritually exhilarating. It is a must have for every youth worker to use, either in group discussions, seminars or straightforward teaching. This piece of work will yet raise the gospel abroad.

Reviewer: **Dr M Akindele**, Consultant Paediatrician, London, UK

 :www.protokospublishers.co.uk

OTHER BOOKS.

Let's Reason Together ...Youths' A-Z (Book 2)

According to the United Nations demographic statistics, the global youth population, ranging in age from 15 to 24 years, today stands at more than 1.5 billion, representing about 22 percent or a fifth of the world's 6.8 billion people inhabiting the earth. In developing nations where a greater number of this group resides, the youth population sometimes gets as high as 60% or more of the total population of such nations!

Since it is also globally accepted that the youth of any nation forms the strength of that nation, economically, militarily and/or otherwise, it is imperative that this group of people cannot be overlooked.

It is against this backdrop that the book, **LET'S REASON TOGETHER – YOUTH'S A-Z** is a timely one that is set to address the various issues that affect young people as well as their vision and aspirations. Since the primary goal of young people is to live full lives in their societies, this book examines specific elements that would help them in this process. It covers a wide range of issues from the sublime such as anger, drugs, examination, homosexuality, jealousy and rejection to the seemingly mundane such as growth, ignorance and youth etc.

Key Features:
- A relevant word per alphabet.
- A time to reflect on the key word.
- An easy phrase per alphabet to remember.
- 3 prayer points per alphabet to help you pray.

Book details:
Paperback: 322 pages
Language: English
ISBN : 978-0-9557898-9-2

Review:
This is a must read for the youths and anyone that deals with teenagers. All Sunday school staff will benefit from this book.
Reviewer: **Deaconess B. Josiah**. London, UK

 :www.protokospublishers.co.uk

OTHER BOOKS.

OLUWAKEMI O. OLA-OJO

GOOD DADS, BAD DADS

This is a timeless book for men of all generations. It is very pragmatic, informative and honest in its outlook and aims to be some resource of great support and guidance to fathers specifically and men in general.

It tackles such issues as showing favouritism, unconditional love, keeping pledges, providing for the family, building an altar of worship, obedience to God's voice and the importance of leadership in the home among others.

It is a very good indicator for men who want to ensure that peace, love and orderliness reign supreme in their homes and all other endeavours of life they are involved in. It is by no means exhaustive in its nature but acts as a pointer to the ageless truths found in the Bible. It challenges men to be all that they can be for the good of the society they live in and most of all the best fathers any children may ever desire to have. It is based on some Biblical characters, all of whom are very different one from the other with their flaws and areas of excellence in order that the good father today might eschew their short-comings and pursue those aspects of these biblical characters that are worthy.

To ensure that fathers continually transform their lives, there is an accompanying workbook to stimulate them and to keep the nuggets found in this book close to their hearts which in turn reflects in the way they live their lives.

Key Features:
- Written especially for today's father in mind.
- Be blessed as you read about 12 other fathers.
- Learn what makes a father good or bad.
- Explore the pains and gains of fatherhood.
- Learn from the secrets of successful fathers.
- Learn from the failures of unsuccessful fathers.
- Learn what your child/ren and wife want from you.

Book details:
Paperback: 230 pages
Language English
ISBN 978-1-908015-00-6

 :www.protokospublishers.co.uk

Other Books.

Review:

"Just a note to say that the book 'Good Dads Bad Dads' is a powerful and thought-provoking book".

Reviewer: **Prof A. I. Sodeye** - United Kingdom

Review
Primarily, I find the book pleasurable to read and understand. To the spiritually inclined, the book is prophetic and as you read along you get the impression that it is not just discussing a topic, but expressing and bringing to light, real life situations. The book is quite engaging and provides an avenue for readers to reflect and take stock as they read along.

As a pastor, I realise that most of the fatherhood problems were highlighted maturely but factually. The author provides the opportunity to receive fresh insights from what is practicable and on-going in human affairs - duties and responsibilities of fathers. Additionally, the book is appropriate in that, absentee-fathers who are privileged to read or hear from someone who has read the book, would have an opportunity to repent and reduce the number of such men to a negligible few.

Furthermore the book is filled with wisdom and encouragement for anyone doing well as a father and, for those who are not really there yet, the author offers hope, contact details and prayers of repentance. I salute the writer for effective communication on a sensitive topic such as this. The book, 'Good dads, Bad Dads' is not judgemental or sentimental, but it is timely, culturally relevant and once read, you will like to read it again. I recommend this book to all serious dads and to those hoping to be one!

Reviwer: **Pastor Isaac Ajibolorunrin**
Christ The Lord Tabernacle, London UK.

:www.protokospublishers.co.uk

OTHER BOOKS.

GOOD DADS, BAD DADS (Work Book)

This is a timeless book for men of all generations. It is very pragmatic, informative and honest in its outlook and aims to be some resource of great support and guidance to fathers specifically and men in general.

It tackles such issues as showing favouritism, unconditional love, keeping pledges, providing for the family, building an altar of worship, obedience to God's voice and the importance of leadership in the home among others.

It is a very good indication for men who want to ensure that peace, love and orderliness reign supreme in their homes and all other endeavours of life they are involved in. It is not at all exhaustive in its nature but acts as a pointer to the ageless truths found in the Bible. It challenges men to be all that they can be for the good of the society they live in and most of all the best fathers any child(ren) may ever desire to have.

To ensure that fathers continually transform lives, this is the accompanying workbook to stimulate them and to keep the nuggets found close to their hearts which in turn reflects in the way they live their lives.

Key Features:
Essentially for the present day father. This workbook allows you:
- To be encouraged and motivated as a father.
- To use it as an individual or in a men's group.
- Time to reflect on the lives of the 12 fathers you have read.
- Opportunity to identify your own strengths and weakness.
- To have relevant prayer points to help you pray in your role.

Book details:
Paperback : 152 pages
Language : English
ISBN : 978-1-908015-01-3

 :www.protokospublishers.co.uk

OTHER BOOKS.

ABC of PEOPLE and THINGS in the BIBLE

This Workbook 'ABC of People and Things in the Bible' is specifically written for the 6-8 year old as a corresponding tool to help the child learn and practice the lessons taught from the book, ABC of People and Things in the Bible. It provides a series of basic do-it-yourself activities such as reading, writing and drawing.

The workbook is a perfect teaching aid that enables the child to express him/herself and helps the parent/teacher to identify the depth of the child's understanding or otherwise of the lessons taught.

Key Features:
- Hours of learning and fun at the same time.
- Encourage child's self-confidence in reading.
- Encouraging good handwriting through practice.
- Unique and personalized workbook for your child.
- Easy way to monitor's child's developments and creativity
- Opportunity for your child's creativity to be developed/enhanced.

Book details:
Paperback: 64 pages
Language English
ISBN 978-1-908015-05-1

Review:
I love the entire concept - creatively teaching the Bible through Bible stories and creatively teaching how to write in a fun and in an Interactive way.

Reviewer: **O. Ukaejiofo.** UK.

 :www.protokospublishers.co.uk

OTHER BOOKS.

ABC of PEOPLE and THINGS in the BIBLE
(Parent/Teachers Manual 1)

Creative! That is the only word to describe Oluwakemi Ola-Ojo's new book, ABC of People and Things in the Bible. Many Christian parents desire to give their children an early start in Christian living and discipline through the knowledge of the Bible but simply do not know how. The reason for this is not farfetched. Teaching a six-year old is not exactly a dinner date, or is it?

ABC of People and Things in the Bible provides the perfect answer to this challenge.

The book presents a highly efficient way of teaching 6-8 year-olds the Bible in a friendly yet educative manner. Using the letters of the English alphabet, Oluwakemi Ola-Ojo details the lives of people in the Bible, to teach children moral values that will help to shape their lives as well as helping them to identify and avoid mistakes that destroyed the lives of some of the characters mentioned.

The book comes highly recommended as a teaching aid not just in Sunday school but in regular school classes as well as private home studies.

Key Features:
Essentially for the present day Parent/Teacher. This manual allows you:
- To learn at the Creator's feet.
- To learn about many people in the Bible.
- To have wholesome discussions with your child
- To adapt the various teachings to the level of child.
- To teach your child line-upon line, precept –upon - precept
- Gives you many hours of learning and fun together with the child.

Book details:
Paperback: 112 pages
Language: English
ISBN 978-1-908015-04-4

:www.protokospublishers.co.uk

OTHER BOOKS.

ABC of Place and Things in the Bible - Child's Workbook (Age 9-10)

This is a work tool that comes as a complimentary companion to the book, ABC of Places and Things in the Bible. It is an interactive manual designed to assist the child's learning, by providing him/her the opportunity to read and to commit to memory, the contents of the book. The workbook also helps to improve the child's writing and drawing skills, and gives him/her room to explore and express his/her creative ability in any or all of these areas while having fun in the process.

There is no doubt that the workbook is a practical aid to learning for 9-10 year olds. It therefore comes highly recommended.

Key Features:
- Hours of learning and fun at the same time.
- Encourage child's self-confidence in reading.
- Encouraging good handwriting through practice.
- Unique and personalized workbook for your child.
- Easy way to monitor's child's developments and creativity.
- Opportunity for your child's creativity to be developed/enhanced.

Book details:
Paperback: 64 pages
Language: English
ISBN: 978-1-908015-03-7

 :www.protokospublishers.co.uk

OTHER BOOKS.

ABC of Places and Things in the Bible. (Parent/Teachers Manual 1)

ABC of Places and Things in the Bible (Age 9-10) is the second in a series of Kiddies books specifically designed and written by Oluwakemi Ola-Ojo for children of elementary school age. The book comes as a sequel to ABC of People and Things in the Bible (Age 6-8). It seeks to bridge the gap between parents' desire to educate their children on basic Bible teachings and the ability to pass the information to children of such tender ages in a way they would understand and retain, and in addition, in a manner that will make a positive impact on them.

Like the first in the series, the book offers a highly efficient way of teaching 9-10 year-olds the Bible in a friendly and educative manner. Using the letters of the English alphabet, Oluwakemi Ola-Ojo details key places and things in the Bible, to teach children historical and geographical landmarks of interest as well as objects of significance, not only in ancient biblical times, but also in present day 21st Century.

The book will definitely stir up the imagination of every child

Key Features:
Essentially for the present day Parent/Teacher. This manual allows you:
- To learn at the Creator's feet.
- To learn about places and things in the Bible.
- To have wholesome discussions with your child
- To adapt the various teachings to the level of child.
- To teach your child line-upon line, precept –upon - precept
- Gives you many hours of learning and fun together with the child.

Book details:
Paperback: 111 pages
Language: English
ISBN: 978-1-908015-02-0

:www.protokospublishers.co.uk

COMING OUT SOON

- INSPIRATIONS FOR THE MAN OF VALOUR.
- INSPIRATIONS FOR THE MAN OF COURAGE.
- MY A.B.C. OF PEOPLE AND THINGS IN THE BIBLE. (SERIES 2)
- MY ABC OF PLACES AND THINGS (SERIES 2)
- TO THE GROOM WITH LOVE.

USEFUL ADDRESSES & WEBSITES

Care for the Family
PO Box 488
Cardiff
CF15 7YY
Tel: (029) 2081 0800
Fax: (029) 2081 4089
Email: mail@cff.org.uk
Website: www.care-for-the-family.org.uk OR www.cff.org.uk
Care for the Family aims to promote strong family life and to help those hurting because of family breakdown. Their heart is to come alongside people in the good times and in the tough times – bringing hope, compassion and some practical, down-to-earth help and encouragement.

Children Evangelism Ministry Inc
P.O. Box 4480
Ilorin, Kwara State,
Nigeria.
Tel: +234 31 222199
E-mail: cem@ilorin.skannet.com OR cem562000@yahoo.com
Children Evangelism Ministry Inc is a ministry that reaches out with the Gospel to children before and after birth. The ministry teaches and equips parents, teachers and coordinators of Sunday Schools and Children's Clubs. They also have and hold Children's Clubs, conferences and training seminars.

Focus on the Family
Tel: 1-800 - 232 6459
Website: www.family.org
Focus on the Family cooperates with the Holy Spirit in disseminating the Gospel of Jesus Christ to as many people as possible, and, specifically, to accomplish that objective by helping to preserve traditional values and the institution of the family.

Open Gate
2 Union Road
Croydon
CR0 2XU.
Tel: 0208 665 5533
Fax: 0208 684 7233
e-mail: opengate@yahoo.co.uk
         alteschool@yahoo.co.uk
Open Gate Provides a preventative and supplementary educational facility for youths at risk of permanent exclusion. We aim at empowering and connecting the youths for the future. We provide support for the family and the community.

Protokos Publishers
London, UK
www.protokospublishers.co.uk
(Impacting our community through sharing)
Protokos Publishers provides various resources for the family. We publish many life's enlightening, informative and motivational must read books. With each of our books, you are guaranteed a 24/7 counsellor by your side on the subject.

The Shepherd's Ministries
5 Brookehowse Road
Bellingham
London SE6 3TJ, UK
Tel/Fax: +44 208 698 7222
Email: info@theshepherdsministries.org
Website: www.theshepherdsministries.org
The Shepherd's Ministries helps to bring children into an experience of worshipping God in truth and in spirit; give children a world-view based on God's word and mission and helps children to exercise their gifts in local and global missions.

USEFUL ADDRESSES & WEBSITES.

Teenagers' Outreach Ministries (TOM) Inc.
Plot 85
Ladi Kwali Ext. Layout,
P.O.Box 16
Kwali, Abuja.
Nigeria.
Tel- 02082933730
Fax-02082933731
Nigeria - 08037044195, 07081860407
Email- tominthq@yahoo.co.uk
Website -www.tominternational.org
The Teenagers' Outreach Ministries (TOM) Inc. has a vision of leading today's teenager to Christ. This forms the foundation on which we mould their character in line with the word of God, thereby equipping them to fulfil their God ordained roles in life.

Total Woman Ministries
The Total Woman Ministries,
3 Herringham Road
Thames Wharf Barrier,
Charlton,
London
SE7 8NJ.
Tel: 020 8293 3730
Fax: 020 8293 3731
Email: admin@totalwomanministries.org
Website:www.totalwomanministries.org
Total Woman Ministries by God's grace has the sole vision of reaching out to women of all categories *(married, single, separated, divorced, young, middle-aged or elderly).*

United Christian Broadcasting UCB
P.O. Box 255, Stoke on Trent,
ST4 8YY, England
Among other forms of spreading the Gospel, UCB prints The Word For Today – a free daily devotional reading available for residents in the UK and Republic of Ireland

IN USA:
www.eCounseling.com
Tel Number: 1-866-268-6735

www.ingramcontent.com/pod-product-compliance
Lightning Source LLC
Chambersburg PA
CBHW070951080526
44587CB00015B/2254